What Christian Living Is All About

Studies in James

Rubel Shelly

21st Century Christian

ISBN 0-89098-023-3
ISBN -13 978-0-89098-023-1

Table of Contents

Foreword

There is no more practical book in all the Bible than the epistle of James. Its theme is sounded at 1:27 where *pure and faultless religion* is mentioned. It is about the day-to-day living of one's religion. It contains the kind of exhortation and encouragement that Christians need to hear constantly, for it shows us how to take our religion with us when we leave the church building. In the most helpful terms possible, James tells us *What Christian Living is All About.*

No sincere Christian can read and study this epistle without spiritual growth taking place. This means that James is especially important to young Christians who are attempting to get their lives on course with their Savior's will. You need to master the lessons in James concerning the discouragement you are likely to feel at times because of challenges to your faith, about equality before God, regarding the use of your tongue, about prayer, and so on. Every sentence in the epistle will be helpful to you -- if you will be a doer of the word and not just a hearer (cf. James 1:22).

The book you are reading now is designed to help you study, appreciate, and apply the important lessons in James. It is not a work of great scholarly merit. It is not a commentary. It is not the last word on anything in James. It is merely one tool for you to use in studying this important piece of God-breathed literature. Use as many other tools and helpful study materials as you can find, and go as deeply into the epistle of James as you can. Every new discovery and insight into this marvelous little section of the New Testament will thrill and encourage you.

Under thirteen topical headings, this book examines every verse in the entire epistle. It then expands the study of the subject at hand by introducing other Bible passages which bear on the same theme. An effort is then made to apply what the Word of God has said on these subjects to the immediate needs of people living in our challenging and exciting time in history.

For the 1989 revision of *What Christian Living is All About,* I owe special gratitude to Teresa Stephens for retyping the original manuscript and to Diana Gilfilen for helping me edit and proofread the revised manuscript for publication.

My sincere prayer is that your study of the Word of God with the aid of this little book will contribute greatly to your ability to live the Christian experience faithfully and joyously all the days of your life.

Rubel Shelly

Chapter 1

A Special Man and a Special Book
James 1:1

The little book of James is one of the most practical pieces of sacred literature. Moreover, it remains fully as practical for the twentieth century as it was for the first century.

Do men still have trials and temptations to face? Are obstacles of prejudice and discrimination ever found among brethren of differing economic or social levels? Do some people want only to profess faith without actually living it? Does anyone's tongue ever get out of control? Is worldliness ever found among the people of God?

So long as there are human beings living on this planet, problems such as these will exist. Just that long do men need to read and study the book of James, then, for it gives inspired counsel which guides Christians through these hindrances to mature faith.

The message of James is appropriate to Christians of every period in history. Its theme is sounded in 1:27 where *pure and faultless religion* is mentioned. "Religion that God our Father accepts as pure and faultless is this: to look after orphans and widows in their distress and to keep oneself from being polluted by the world."

With this key statement, James lets his readers know that the Christian religion is founded on *compassion* (i.e., looking after widows and orphans) and *purity* (i.e., avoiding the world's moral pollution). So this epistle is about the day-to-day living of one's religion. It is the kind of exhortation that members of Christ's body need to hear constantly, for it shows how to take religion with you when you leave the church building. It appeals for Christians to let our religion really make a difference in the way we live.

James shows, in the most practical way possible, *what Christian living is all about*. It is a very special book which deserves unhurried and frequent study. Applying its teachings to our lives will cause us to be "doers of the word and not hearers only" (James 1:22 KJV). Heeding the instructions of this inspired epistle will turn half-hearted Christians into truly consecrated and faithful disciples of the Lord Jesus Christ.

The Author of the Epistle

The final author of every word in the Bible is the Holy Spirit. The setting forth of the will of God in both the Old and New Testaments was accomplished as "men spoke from God as they were carried along by the Holy Spirit" (2 Pet. 1:21). Thus it is our responsibility to acknowledge the authority of this body of writings and to receive it "not as the word of men, but as it actually is, the word of God, which is at work in you who believe" (1 Thess. 2:13).

But the fact nevertheless remains that this inspired, complete, and authoritative revelation of truth was delivered to us through men. These men were somehow supervised by the Spirit of God so that they could not destroy or mar the message being given through them. Their very words were chosen by the Holy Spirit and not by themselves (cf. 1 Cor. 2:12-16).

All this does not mean, however, that the men used for this task of communicating truth were incidental and unimportant as persons. Not at all. Their individuality and personality were not eliminated by the Holy Spirit. In fact, they were chosen for certain tasks of revelation because of their background, disposition, and training. For example, Paul wrote as Paul (e.g., vocabulary and style), and Peter wrote as Peter. This makes the process of inspiration all the more amazing. The Holy Spirit could respect and use the individuality of each man and yet so control them all that the result of their work would be his own production.

Due to the fact that James' background and personality are a part of the epistle the Holy Spirit produced through him, it is almost compulsory that we look briefly at the man in order to appreciate the section of Holy Scripture produced through him.

Several men with the name *James* are found in the New Testament record.

There is James the son of Zebedee and brother of John (cf. Matt. 4:21; Mark 1:19; Luke 5:10). Although this James was evidently very close to Jesus -- being among the "select three" (Peter, James and John) who frequently were with Jesus apart from the other apostles (cf. Mark 5:37; Matt. 26:37) -- he did not write this epistle. He died as a martyr in A.D. 44 (cf. Acts 12:1-2), and the book of James was almost certainly written later than this.

There is James the son of Alphaeus (cf. Matt. 10:3; Mark 3:18; Luke 6:15; Acts 1:13). Actually we know nothing of this James except that he was an apostle. So obscure a person could hardly have written this kind of letter, for the epistle of James presupposes that its readers would know its author and heed its counsel accordingly. This same consideration of obscurity weighs against the possibility that the book was written by the James mentioned in Luke 6:16 or by some unknown James.

Thus, by the process of elimination, the most likely possibility for the authorship of this epistle is James the brother of Jesus (cf. Matt. 13:55; Mark 6:3; Gal. 1:19). This view has been the one most generally held by students of the book. This is the only James who played a sufficiently central role in the history of the early church to have qualified for the authorship of this epistle. This would mean that he was the brother of another New Testament writer, Jude (cf. Jude 1).

Scripture tells us that Jesus had four brothers -- James, Joseph, Judas, and Simon. In the two verses which name

11

them (Matt. 13:55; Mark 6:3), the name of James is listed first. This may suggest that he was the oldest of the four and was therefore closest in age to Jesus.

From John 7:3-5 we learn that James, along with the other brothers (actually only half-brothers since their father was Joseph and Jesus' conception was by a miracle), did not believe Jesus' claims about himself. Beyond this, it even appears that he was among those who sought to discourage the Lord in the work of his public ministry among men.

But an altogether different picture of this man is painted in Acts and in the New Testament epistles. An event occurred in his life which thoroughly changed him. It transformed him from a doubter into a disciple. Jesus appeared to James after his resurrection from the dead and thereby dissolved away all his doubts and reservations about the truthfulness of his claims to be the Messiah and Son of God (cf. 1 Cor. 15:7). So immediate a change of heart was produced in James that, whereas he was an unbeliever at the close of the Gospel narratives, he was numbered among the believers in Jerusalem when the book of Acts begins (Acts 1:14).

It is clear that from this point on James advanced to become a leading figure in the church at Jerusalem. When Peter was released from prison by an angel and rejoined some of the brethren at the home of Mary, the mother of John Mark, he told them the details of his miraculous deliverance and said, "Tell James and the brothers about this" (Acts 12:17b). When the apostles and elders met to discuss the question of Gentile admission to the church, it was James who made the final and definitive statement on the matter (Acts 15:13ff). Paul reported his labors to James upon his return from the third missionary journey (Acts 21:18-25). He referred to him in one of his epistles as one of the "pillars" of the church at Jerusalem (Gal. 2:9).

Non-biblical history informs us that James was known as "the Just" because of his many virtues. Eusebius says he spent so much time in prayer on his knees that his knees "grew worn and hard, like those of a camel."

What a difference was made in the life of James by the power of a living faith. He had grown up in the same house with Jesus. He had witnessed his sinless life and had heard many of his wonderful teachings. But he had been a stumbling block to Jesus' cause until he underwent the radical change which resulted from the evidence of his brother's resurrection.

You should not overlook that, in beginning this epistle, James identified himself as "a servant of God and of the Lord Jesus Christ." This self-identification is both an evidence of the humility of the man and a recognition that one's spiritual relationship to Christ, not his fleshly relationship, is the crucial matter (cf. Mark 3:31-35).

Background to the Epistle

Having shown that James was a "special man" (i.e., by virtue of his association with Jesus and his experiences in the early church) whom God chose for the writing of this epistle, think next about how the epistle itself constitutes a "special book" to us as we study the Word of God.

New Testament epistles were produced for specific people with definite purposes in mind. They are permanently valuable because their authors were guided by the Holy Spirit. It would be rather naive to think that James was assigned a five-chapter section of the New Testament to write and sat down to dash it off for the printers. No, he wrote this epistle to people for whom he felt a sense of personal responsibility. He exhorted them in very much the same way a father would exhort his children -- with both authority and love.

And just who were the people to whom this letter was originally written? James wrote "to the twelve tribes scattered among the nations." Although some have suggested this might be an address to Christians in general -- both Jews and Gentiles -- under the figure of the church as spiritual Israel, it is more likely an address to Jewish Christians who had been forced to flee Jerusalem and for whom James had a great personal concern.

The readers had been "scattered" because of an intense persecution against Jewish Christians. "On that day a great persecution broke out against the church at Jerusalem, and all except the apostles were scattered throughout Judea and Samaria" (Acts 8:1; cf. 12:1ff). When these saints had lived in Jerusalem, they had looked to James as their teacher and counselor. They were now separated from him, and the pain of heart over this situation was mutual.

James knew of the severe trials which these saints were undergoing (cf. James 1:2) and desired to help them by strengthening their faith, increasing their courage, and warning them against spiritual indifference.

A simple outline of the epistle which you might find helpful in your study follows:

The Salutation (1:1)
I. Pure Religion in a Time of Trial. 1:1-18.
    A. A positive attitude toward trials (1:2-4)
    B. How to face trials successfully (1:5-11)
       1. Prayer (1:5-8)
       2. Awareness of life's true value (1:9-11)
    C. God blesses those who endure (1:12)
II. How Faith is Tested in the World. 1:19-5:18.
    A. Its reaction to God's Word (1:19-27)
    B. Relations with others (2:1-13)
    C. Right actions (2:14-26)
    D. Control of the tongue (3:1-18)
    E. Avoiding worldliness and strife (4:1-12)
    F. Acknowledging God's will (4:13-17)
    G. Reacting to oppression (5:1-12)
    H. Its dependence on prayer (5:13-18)
III. On Restoring Fallen Brothers. 5:19-20.
    A. Some will fall (5:19)
    B. The importance of reclaiming them (5:20)

Since the epistle appears to have been written after the persecutions of A.D. 33 and 41, it must be dated in the mid-40s at the earliest. Furthermore, in light of the fact that the controversy over receiving Gentiles into the church (A.D. 48) seems not to be an issue in it, it likely was not written past the mid-point of the century. Thus we will say James was written sometime around A.D. 45.

If this date is accepted, it means that James is likely the first of all 27 New Testament books to have been written.

Reacting to James

You can imagine the enthusiasm with which this epistle was received. The scattering of Christians from Jerusalem had taken place in A.D. 35 (Acts 8) and A.D. 44 (Acts 12). Thus some of these people had not seen or had any direct word from James in ten or more years. Others were only recently separated from him. How excited they all must have been to have word from their beloved brother and teacher. How practical they would have found his counsel to be.

We can read James today with equal enthusiasm and interest, for this book is eminently down-to-earth and sensible. It tells us how to conform our attitudes, speech, and behavior to the will of God so we can be the light of the world and the salt of the earth.

Conclusion

The time that you are willing to devote to this study will be rewarded with an understanding of some exciting biblical truths.

Every verse in the short epistle will be studied in these thirteen lessons. Emphasis will be given both to the historical setting and original meaning of each exhortation in the book and to the present-day application of these inspired instructions.

The following plan of study will reward you richly: (1) read the entire epistle of James at least twice each week -- this will require about five minutes of reading per day, (2) study each chapter in this book carefully before attending class each week, (3) pray for God's help in learning the great truths of this epistle, and (4) look for daily opportunities to practice the pure religion described in James.

Learn the lessons of this New Testament epistle and you will know *what Christian living is all about.*

Memorize Matthew 5:10-12

TAKE THOUGHT

1. Discuss the nature of *inspiration*. Give emphasis to the fact that its purpose was to guarantee an infallible revelation of the will of God to man. Read John 14:26; 16:13; Acts 2; 2 Tim. 3:16-17.

2. Contrast the picture of James in the Gospels with that in Acts and the epistles. What crucial event led to this transformation?

3. A very interesting thing about this epistle is an amazing similarity between its teachings and those of Jesus in the Sermon on the Mount. Compare the following examples and try to find others: James 1:2 and Matt. 5:10-12; James 1:5 and Matt. 7:7ff; James 1:20 and Matt. 5:22; James 1:22 and Matt. 7:24ff, etc.

4. What specific and immediate need occasioned the writing of this epistle? Show that the themes treated in it are relevant to our time.

5. Martin Luther referred to James as "an epistle of straw" and placed it at the very end of his translation of the New Testament. He held this view because he thought James contradicted Paul's teaching on salvation by faith. Evaluate this view. Cf. Gal. 2:16; James 2:24; Gal. 5:6.

TAKE ACTION

1. Check the church library to see what study aids on James are available to you. Familiarize yourself with these books and use them in your research and study during this quarter.

2. Make an earnest attempt to get people who should be attending this class but who are neglecting Bible study to participate in the study of James you are beginning today.

3. Read through the book of James at one sitting to "get the feel" of it. Decide on the best time for you to do your daily reading of the epistle and your weekly study of this book. Pray for God to help you stay with your schedule.

Chapter 2

Problems, Problems, Problems!
James 1:2-8, 12-15

Ever get the feeling that life is a constant series of problems?

There is always some crisis to be faced, some hard decision to make, some hurt to be absorbed, some bill to be paid, or some illness or accident from which to recover. Or it may be that the problem arises from an entirely opposite situation. The healthy man who is working hard every day and doing well in his business or profession may become so successful that he is under constant pressure to keep production and profits up. His success, wealth, and popularity expose him to problems that create ulcers and cause heart attacks for many others like him. You see, everyone has his own special problems.

Oh, you might say that you would rather have the "problems" of the talented and popular person over those of the person who stands lower on the ladder of success and popularity. But my point is simply that everybody does have problems -- not just you.

Problems, problems, problems! Won't they ever go away? Why must these things happen to people? At least, why must they happen to Christians?

A Positive View of Problems

The Bible encourages us not to think of these things in negative terms. God wants us to take a positive view of our problems. He wants us to allow even the most trying experiences to produce a good effect in our lives. This will take some readjustment of our thinking, but it is worth the effort.

The Holy Spirit gave us this message through James: "Consider it pure joy, my brothers, whenever you face trials of many kinds. . . . Blessed is the man who perseveres under trial, because when he has stood the test, he will receive the crown of life that God has promised to those who love him" (James 1:2, 12).

Don't whine, cry, and give way to despair when you have a difficult situation to face or a hard problem to solve. Celebrate! Sing! Rejoice!

What? Celebrate because you've got problems? No. Celebrate because you have a loving and powerful Lord who will bring you through your problems and turn them into stepping stones towards your spiritual maturity. Sing because you are not alone. Rejoice in the knowledge that you don't have to let things get the best of you.

The Meaning of "Temptation" in James 1

The Greek word translated "temptation" in older versions of the first chapter of James can have two different meanings.

As with our English word, it can refer to external stresses and trials that press upon us or to internal attractions to do wrong. James uses the word in both ways in this chapter, and this distinction of meaning must be remembered as we study it. The Revised Standard and New International Versions employ the helpful device of using the word "trial" when it is used in the former sense and "temptation" when it is used in the latter sense.

James refers to *life's external trials* in verses 2, 3, and 12. Such things as sorrow, sickness, pain, disappointment, hardship, and grief are referred to here.

Consider the trials James' original readers were experiencing when this letter was written. They had been forced to leave their homes in Jerusalem under persecution (Acts 8:1). They were living in places new to them and among strangers (James 1:1). They were having to adjust to an entirely different life. These things were testing the faithful-

18

ness of James' readers. Would these Hebrew Christians remain faithful to Christ and the church? Would they decide that too much was being asked of them and give up?

Such trials have always come upon the people of God to give them an opportunity to prove their faith (i.e., trust) in the Lord. They are still here and always shall be. We are tried daily by the changing values of our world, the conflicts of racial tension, the distress of inflation, the ever-present threat of nuclear annihilation, betrayal by "friends," and crushed dreams. These strains and stresses are common to all of us. They test our moral and spiritual quality.

Every man or woman is regarded as unproven before God, and the "trials of many kinds" come to put everyone to the test. These trials are not evil in themselves, and God is not blameworthy for allowing them. The high winds and rains of a storm are not evil, yet some houses do fall. They fall because their structures are weak and haven't had adequate reinforcement against storms. In the same way the common trials of life are not evil, yet some people do fall and break under them. They do so because they did not build on a solid rock and allow the Spirit of God to reinforce their characters with his strength (cf. Matt. 7:24-27).

James next focuses attention on *temptations designed to lead people into sin.* These are not the same as the everyday stresses and strains of life. These are sinister in nature and intend to do us harm. This sort of temptation is treated beginning at verse 13: "When tempted, no one should say, 'God is tempting me.' For God cannot be tempted by evil, nor does he tempt anyone."

While it is true that God proves the real character of men by subjecting them to various tests of their faith (cf. Abraham, Gen. 22:1), it is not true that he seduces men into evil. Let no man blame his sin or the circumstances which led to it on God.

Adam was, in effect, blaming God for his sin when he said, "The woman you put here with me, she gave me some

19

fruit from the tree, and I ate it" (Gen. 3:12). James answers all such charges as these by asserting the holiness of God. God and evil are eternally opposed to each other. Not only can God not be charmed by evil but he also cannot be responsible for our temptation to do evil. How so? If God could tempt us with evil, he would cease to be holy and thus would cease to be God. For example, could one whom you thought to be a good man still have your esteem if it were proved that he had been selling drugs to children? How could we regard God as good if he brought evil (i.e., sin) into our lives?

What, then, is the source of temptations to do evil? "But each one is tempted when, by his own evil desire, he is dragged away and enticed" (James 1:14). The blame for sin belongs not on God but on man. We do not like to take this responsibility. Mankind generally blames fate or society or circumstance for his immoral and criminal acts. But not so. We do not do as we do because we cannot do otherwise. We are morally free and do wrong because we choose to do wrong. Our "evil desires" (i.e., improper and uncontrolled desires) draw us into sin. Even in situations where we lose our wills and become so addicted to something (e.g., alcohol) that we cannot break the cycle without help, the initial decision to expose ourselves to that enslaving thing was a choice rooted in our own desires.

Someone has illustrated the nature of temptation after this fashion. Suppose a mother fish is being followed by her offspring. All is well and everyone is happy. But then one of the little fishes sees a juicy worm. Mother has said for everyone to stay in line and not to turn aside for anything, but why should he not dart over and gobble up the worm and then get back in place? Will anyone ever know? He is thus drawn off his straight course by an unchecked desire to eat the worm. Now all is lost, for the worm was only bait for a sharp hook.

In the same way, all is well with a man so long as he follows the God of his salvation without turning aside to the right hand or the left. As surely as he sees something out in the world for which he must veer off his straight course to get, however, he goes and gets it only to be caught by it. Unchecked desire within his own heart -- not fate, circumstance, or God -- caused him to sin.

Thus it is that we face problems of two vastly different types. We have trials (i.e., the ordinary events of life which tax our energies) which are part of the divinely created reality of life on earth. These trials are not sinister in character but are allowed to discipline and improve our characters (cf. Heb. 12:11). On the other hand, we have temptations (i.e., enticements to sin) which arise from our own uncontrolled desires. God did not create us with a proneness to sin but with freedom of choice. Our use of this freedom to do wrong is in no way an indictment against God, for he could not have created us as men without giving such freedom. The lack of freedom of will would have made us mere robots and would have made righteousness meaningless. If we did right only because we could not do otherwise, of what value would such right conduct be in bringing glory to God?

How to Overcome Trials and Temptations

We have to live with the problems which grow out of trials and temptations. Beyond that, we have to overcome them by the grace of God. Trials must be endured with patience and grace. Temptations must be conquered with faith and obedience.

How shall we achieve such a victory?

First, we can be *optimistic about the struggle*. "Consider it pure joy . . ." We can afford to rejoice in the confidence inspired by this promise: "No temptation has seized you except what is common to man. And God is faithful; he will not let you be tempted beyond what you can bear. But when

21

you are tempted, he will also provide a way out so that you can stand up under it" (1 Cor. 10:13).

An attitude of pessimistic fatalism will almost certainly mean failure. Get your chin up off the ground. Lift your eyes heavenward in optimistic confidence. You can make it, for you have God's promise of help.

Second, *pray that God will meet your daily needs* out of his infinite supply of mercy. Do you need answers to questions? Do you need help in making a right decision? Do you feel confused and sense a need for wisdom and understanding to react to your trials and temptations in the right way? "If any of you lacks wisdom, he should ask God, who gives generously to all without finding fault, and it will be given to him" (James 1:5).

When a Christian prays such a prayer, he must pray it in full confidence that an answer will be forthcoming. He must believe that God can and will help him bear his burden and stay on the right course. "But when he asks, he must believe and not doubt, because he who doubts is like a wave of the sea, blown and tossed by the wind. That man should not think he will receive anything from the Lord; he is a double-minded man, unstable in all he does" (James 1:6-8). Most of our doubts in prayer are attributable to a divided heart -- i.e., being "double-minded" and "unstable." We want God's blessings and power in our lives, but we don't want to make the necessary sacrifices or changes in our lives that are required in order to be conformed to his will. This type of prayer gets no answer.

Third, in the case of temptations to evil, it helps to resist them when you *remember the outcome of sin*. "Then, after desire has conceived, it gives birth to sin; and sin, when it is full-grown, gives birth to death" (James 1:15). There is no future in sin. Its course is inevitably downward. Uncontrolled desire becomes an evil deed which (if unforgiven) brings spiritual death. "Then death and Hades were thrown into the lake of fire. The lake of fire is the second death"

(Rev. 20:14). What an awful fate. What a high price to pay for sin.

The Reward for Those Who Overcome
The greatest incentive one can have to overcome his trials and temptations is his awareness of the reward promised those who endure and conquer.

First, there is the spiritual maturity which comes from the experience. "Because you know that the testing of your faith develops perseverance. Perseverance must finish its work so that you may be mature and complete, not lacking anything" (James 1:3-4). A Christian does not become spiritually mature and strong overnight. He is not "born of water and the Spirit" (John 3:5) one day and found to be a full-grown man the next day. Growth takes place gradually -- through the testing of faith -- and requires patience. Allowed to have its full effect, patient endurance of trials will make one mature (i.e., fully developed) and complete (i.e., with no unfinished part).

Second, the man or woman who endures trials and overcomes temptations "will receive *the crown of life* that God has promised to those who love him" (James 1:12b). The life promised here stands in stark contrast to the death which comes as the result of sin (James 1:15). It is what the Bible calls "eternal life" -- a new quality of life in the present age and then life with God amidst the splendors of heaven when this world has passed away. In reflecting on the problems of life in relation to a promised home in heaven for overcoming them, one could join with Paul to say, "I consider that our present sufferings are not worth comparing with the glory that will be revealed in us" (Rom. 8:18).

Conclusion
What is Christian living all about? It is not a fleeting moment of religious excitement in a darkened room which

transports one beyond this world or makes her oblivious to it. It is the development of an obedient, realistic, and practical faith that will enable a believer to take up his cross, follow Jesus daily, and rejoice in the grace of God which shows itself from hour to hour -- from problem to problem -- in his life.

Memorize James 1:12

TAKE THOUGHT
    1. What usually comes to mind when you hear the word "temptation"? In what two ways is the word used in James 1?
    2. How do people ordinarily react to their problems? How does God want Christian to react to ours?
    3. God allowed Joseph to be sent into Egypt and to go through a series of trying episodes (cf. Gen. 45:5-8). Did God do this to destroy Joseph or to develop him? What was the outcome of it all? What if Joseph had abandoned God and given way to fleshly passion with Potiphar's wife?
    4. Study the following verses about overcoming temptations to sin: Matt. 6:13; 1 Thess. 5:22; Rom. 14:23. What primary insight comes to you from each of them?
    5. Discuss the rewards promised to those who overcome their problems. Would it be better to live without problems of any kind in this life? Or do we need the discipline which comes of having to face them?

TAKE ACTION
    1. Spend some time this week visiting in a hospital or nursing home. Be observant to the attitudes of these people toward their problems. Try to encourage and lift the spirits of those who do not have a positive attitude. Remind them of God's concern for them, and let them feel your own genuine concern.
    2. Concentrate on the one greatest temptation which you have to overcome. Why does this particular thing attract you? What have you done to strengthen yourself against it? What do you need to do yet?
    3. Much of the excitement and emotionalism of alleged *glossalalia* (i.e., speaking in tongues) is traceable to the effort of people to find a quick escape from tensions and life problems. Secure a copy of *The Psychology of Speaking in Tongues* by John P. Kildahl and read pages 57-59 and 78. Then read the last paragraph of this chapter again and discuss the matter in detail.

24

Chapter 3

Where All Men Are Equal
James 1:9-11; 2:1-13

The problem of prejudice and respect of persons has to be faced afresh by every generation. In days gone by, the problem was between rich and poor, Jew and Gentile, Roman and barbarian. Today it is between rich and poor, management and labor, white and black, educated and uneducated. The problem is still here, and each of us has to face it in the particular circumstances of his own life.

The word "prejudice" literally refers to the pre-judgment of another. Without really knowing the person or having sufficient knowledge of him to form an intelligent opinion, one judges him -- because of his race, economic status, or some other outward circumstance of life -- an unworthy or evil person and denies him his rights. This is snobbery at the least and may even be a form of idolatry.

The disposition to elevate some to positions of eminence in the church and to relegate to the realm of obscurity 'the brother of low degree,' is wholly opposed to the spirit of Christianity and exceedingly wicked in the eyes of God. . . . Some of the most effective work being done for Christ today is by humble, sacrificing servants of the Lord who labor in his cause for sheer love of him, and without desire for public acclaim whatsoever. These, though they may not experience the heady thrill of notoriety characteristic of the more prominent brethren, will nevertheless shine above the brightness of the stars in eternity (Dan. 12:3)." (Guy N. Woods, *A Commentary on the Epistle of James*, pp. 45-46).

Behind the lines in World War I, rest houses were operated which were designed to serve as places of fellowship for all soldiers -- whether officers or enlisted men. Over the entrance of such houses were posted these words: "Abandon all rank, ye who enter here." So must it be in the church. The things which serve to classify and separate men in the world must not be allowed to divide them in the church. "There is neither Jew nor Greek, slave nor free, male nor female, for you are all one in Christ Jesus" (Gal. 3:28).

The Nature of Equality in Christ

Equality is one of those states about which we talk much and know little. The Declaration of Independence declares that all men are created equal. Various laws have been passed to insure the civil rights of all American citizens. Yet we know that absolute human equality in society at large is an impossibility. Graduates from the same class begin with seemingly "equal opportunities" but come to vastly different ends in life. Even if men could be guaranteed equal training, equal opportunities for success in a profession, and equal protection under the law, intangible factors of desire and perseverance would bring them to different levels of achievement and success.

There is one place -- and only one -- where all men are truly equal. That one place is *in Christ*. "The brother in humble circumstances ought to take pride in his high position. But the one who is rich should take pride in his low position, because he will pass away like a wild flower. For the sun rises with scorching heat and withers the plant; its blossom falls and its beauty is destroyed. In the same way, the rich man will fade away even while he goes about his business" (James 1:9-11).

One of the most common bases of social distinction is the disparity of wealth among men. Most of the earliest Christians were apparently of humble status (1 Cor. 1:26; Col. 3:22). Yet there were some among them who were wealthy (Acts 4:34-37; 21:8). James did not require that a communistic state of economic equality be established among these brethren. But the Holy Spirit did cause him to require that such differences not be the basis of discrimination.

The "brother in humble circumstances" (i.e., the Christian who is poor with regard to the treasure which is of the world) is to "take pride in his high position" (i.e., his share in the spiritual treasure which is God's free gift to him). The poor man may be prone to view himself as a failure whose very being is without value. But in Christ this same man sees himself differently and comes to have a new sense of worth and self-esteem. He is important to God (John 3:16; Luke 4:16-21). He is important to the world (Matt. 5:16; 28:19-20). He has every privilege which belongs to children in the family of God (Rom. 8:16-17).

On the other hand, the rich man is to rejoice "in his low position, because he will pass away like a wild flower." In other words, he learns that his material riches are not able to buy spiritual security. He recognizes that his right relationship to God is available only in Christ. He thus obeys the same commandments unto salvation which the poor man obeys and uses his possessions for the glory of God (cf. Matt. 6:19-20; Gal. 6:6-10).

Assuming that a certain poor man and a certain rich man come to see themselves in true perspective and bow in mutual submission before their Lord, there is still the problem of their treatment by other brethren in the church. Will some be tempted to show partiality toward one over the other? Undoubtedly. Thus James addresses himself to this aspect of the problem. "My brothers, as believers in our glorious Lord Jesus Christ, don't show favoritism" (James 2:1). The command is this: Don't try to be a Christian while showing partiality to men. It is strong language.

Does this rule out special friendships? Does this mean that one must never refuse to associate with anyone who wants to be with him? Not at all. Christians *must discriminate* among their associates, but *they must do so on spiritual rather than carnal grounds*. For example, "Do not make friends with a hot-tempered man; do not associate with one easily angered" (Prov. 22:24). Do you refuse friendship to

27

a good man because he does not live in as nice a house as you do or because his skin is of a different color? No. But neither do you form your closest friendships and spend your time with someone who has a bad temper and a wicked tongue. It is necessary to discriminate among people, but you do so for the right reasons.

Some other verses which speak of a proper type of discrimination should also be noted here: "Do not be misled: 'Bad company corrupts good character' " (1 Cor. 15:33). "The elders who direct the affairs of the church well are worthy of double honor, especially those whose work is preaching and teaching" (1 Tim. 5:17).

> Having seen that all are *equal* before God, and that it is sinful to show respect of persons from worldly considerations, inasmuch as every disciple is entitled to the same privileges in Christ (Gal. 3:26-29), it is an extension of this beyond proper bounds to imply that there are no differences obtaining between men. The New Testament teaches us to "honor the king" (1 Pet. 2:13), and to pray for those in high places (1 Tim. 2:2).
>
> Elders, deacons, aged men and women, dignitaries, men of great faith and courage, are often singled out in the Scriptures, and declared to be worthy of special reward for their works of faith, their labors of love, and patience of hope they exhibit. (1 Tim. 5:17; 3:13; 1 Tim. 5:1-3; Heb. 11:1ff; 2 Pet. 2:10,11.) What is taught is that there is no place for worldly acclaim in Christianity, and that all such reverence in public worship is unseemly and sinful. Inasmuch as God is no respecter of persons, neither should we be. (Woods, *op.cit.*, pp. 106-7).

An example of improper discrimination among brethren is cited by James. "Suppose a man comes into your meeting wearing a gold ring and fine clothes, and a poor man in shabby clothes also comes in. If you show special attention to the man wearing fine clothes and say, 'Here's a good seat for you,' but say to the poor man, 'You stand there' or 'Sit on the floor by my feet,' have you not discriminated among yourselves and become judges with evil thoughts?" (James 2:2-4).

The strict caste system of the Roman world created a number of social problems in the early church. That such a situation as the one envisioned in this text should have come about in many assemblies of the saints is not difficult to believe. If you were ushering for a church assembly today and two men came in who fit the general description of the ones mentioned in this passage, would you be prone to show one to a good seat and take the other to a corner in the rear of the auditorium?

In first-century churches composed of poor and humble people, there was a temptation to regard the conversion of a rich or otherwise prominent man as a special event and to make a fuss over him. But there can be no such distinctions of wealth, rank, race, or prestige in the church. Neither can there be discrimination in reverse where a wealthy or influential man in the community is treated contemptuously and "put in his place" by the church.

Thus it was that one could walk into a church assembly in the first century and find a master and slave sitting side-by-side or a slave leading the assembly in which his master sat. Equivalent situations are seen in assemblies of the saints today.

James moves next to specify another reason why Christians should not treat the poor with contempt and stroke the rich. For one thing, since God loves and honors the poor man by giving him access into the kingdom of heaven, it is incongruous that God's people should treat that same person with contempt. Furthermore, he points out that the rich within any culture are more likely to be hostile to the people of Christ.

James makes his points with these words: "Listen, my dear brothers: Has not God chosen those who are poor in the eyes of the world to be rich in faith and to inherit the kingdom he promised those who love him? But you have insulted the poor. Is it not the rich who are exploiting you? Are they not the ones who are dragging you into court? Are they not the ones who are slandering the noble name of him to whom you belong?" (James 2:5-7).

The point is therefore made with forceful emphasis that the people of God are not to be guilty of the sin of partiality. The church of Christ must be the one place where worldly standards of judgment and discrimination are abandoned. Spiritual brotherhood in Christ has made Christians one and has established "peace to men on whom his favor rests" (Luke 2:14; cf. Eph. 2:14).

Living by "The Royal Law"

Christians are never to show favoritism to rich men over poor men or in other ways to become guilty of carnal and unspiritual partiality. To the contrary, we are to live by a higher and nobler standard. We are to observe "the royal law" -- a law which originates with King Jesus and is bound upon all within his kingdom. "If you really keep the royal law found in Scripture, 'Love your neighbor as yourself,' you are doing right. But if you show favoritism, you sin and are convicted by the law as lawbreakers" (James 2:8-10)

To acknowledge the fundamental rightness of this important commandment about loving one's neighbor as himself and then to turn around and show partiality is to sin. To say, in effect, that you will love your neighbor but choose your neighbors carefully is foolish. We are not entitled to pick those whom we will regard as neighbors and look down our noses at the rest of mankind.

The Jews of Jesus' day told themselves that they were obligated only to others of their own race and then only to those who were on an equivalent social plane. Thus they would love their neighbors -- if those neighbors were "their own kind." Jesus gave the Parable of the Good Samaritan to rebuke this narrow attitude. The Samaritan rendered aid to a man who was a stranger. He was of another race and religion. Thereby the Samaritan proved himself to be a real neighbor to the man in need. Jesus concluded the parable with these words: "Go and do likewise" (Luke 10:25-37).

But men will always try to excuse themselves from such obligations, so James posed a possible objection which some might raise to this teaching. Some of the Jews had been prone to regard the law of God as a series of isolated injunctions. To keep one was to gain credit and to break one was to incur debt. Thus a man could add and subtract until he arrived at a reasonable credit for himself. And some of those people had evidently brought that foolish notion into the church with them. Thus he wrote: "For whoever keeps the whole law and yet stumbles at just one point is guilty of breaking all of it. For he who said, 'Do not commit adultery,' also said, 'Do not murder.' If you do not commit adultery but do commit murder, you have become a law-breaker" (James 2:10-11).

James taught that the will of God is one great whole and that to break any part of it is to come under its condemnation. For example, a man is a criminal in a society if he breaks only one law. He does not have to break every statute on the books. So it is with the law of God. One is a sinner whenever he violates any part of God's holy will. Viewed in this light, the sin of partiality is hardly a trivial matter.

This section of the book is then closed with an appeal for Christians to remember that we shall be judged by the law of God. Those who want to receive divine mercy in the final day must show mercy to their neighbors now. "Speak and act as those who are going to be judged by the law that gives freedom, because judgment without mercy will be shown to anyone who has not been merciful. Mercy triumphs over judgment!" (James 2:12-13; cf. Matt. 5:7).

Bible Teaching About Partiality

The book of James is not the only part of the Bible with very pointed teaching about respect of persons. The Old

31

Testament forbids respect of persons. "Do not pervert justice; do not show partiality to the poor or favoritism to the great, but judge your neighbor fairly" (Lev. 19:15).

The New Testament treats this theme extensively. For example, the events related to the conversion of Cornelius were used to teach a lesson to Peter. That lesson, stated in words from Peter's own mouth, was this: "I now realize how true it is that God does not show favoritism but accepts men from every nation who fear him and do what is right" (Acts 10:34-35). Paul affirmed the very same truth in such verses as Romans 2:11 and Colossians 3:25. But, as in the case with every Christian virtue, we see impartiality among men best exemplified in the life of our Lord Jesus Christ.

Jesus neither overlooked the evils of important men nor turned men away because they were unimportant in the eyes of the world. His concern was to save the souls of men and he refused to be distracted from that purpose by considerations of men's worldly status. He was willing to converse with and teach Nicodemus, a "member of the Jewish ruling council" (John 3:1ff), but was equally willing to teach and thereby offer salvation to the outcasts of his society (Luke 15:1-2).

Neither was Jesus' behavior toward others marred by the terrible racial prejudice which so frequently showed itself among his contemporaries (cf. John 4:6-9). Even his worst enemies were forced to admit his impartiality in dealing with men and said: "Teacher, we know that you are true, and care for no man; for you do not regard the position of men, but truly teach the way of God" (Mark 12:15 RSV).

Jesus taught his followers to have the same attitude of impartiality that he showed. He commanded us to treat others as we would want to be treated (Matt. 7:12). Since none of us would want to be the victim of another's prejudice or unfounded fears, none of us can afford to be guilty of treating someone else that way.

Conclusion

Is James a practical book? Does it speak to the needs of modern man? No honest reader can doubt it for a moment.

What is Christian living all about? It involves taking men who have been set right with God through their salvation from sin and setting them right with each other. It shows us how to overcome prejudice in our individual lives and within congregations of the people of God. This lesson must be learned well if we are to evangelize the world and properly represent our impartial God to a color-conscious, class-conscious world.

Memorize: Matthew 7:12

TAKE THOUGHT

1. James has been called the "Amos of the New Testament." Amos was one of the Old Testament prophets who had much to say about social injustice. Read Amos 5:11-15 and see how the sentiment of this passage harmonizes with the section of James studied in today's lesson.

2. The point was made in today's lesson that not all distinctions are evil. Spiritual distinctions among men are not only right but necessary. For example, although God is not a respecter of persons, will all be saved? Why not? Because of racial origins or economic status? Or because of their response to his will? Similarly, Christians must avoid carnal prejudice and fleshly distinctions but make certain spiritual distinctions. What are some of the justifiable distinctions that Christians are obliged to make?

3. Read and discuss the Parable of the Good Samaritan in detail. Suggest some ways in which Christians can be Good Samaritans today.

4. To underscore verse 13 and its teaching concerning merciful treatment of others, read and discuss Matthew 18:21-35.

5. In what situations have you ever been guilty of respect of persons? Do you think you could handle the same situations differently today?

TAKE ACTION

1. Interview someone who is successful in the eyes of the world but who is also a faithful Christian. Ask him to tell you how he regards

his success in business or a profession in comparison to the riches he has in Christ.

2. Interview someone who would not be considered unusually prominent from the world's point of view but who is a faithful Christian. Ask him to tell you his feelings about the spiritual blessings he has in Christ in comparison to fame and wealth. (Note: You will likely be impressed with a similarity of response from the people you interview for questions one and two. What does this tell you about equality in Christ?)

3. What steps can you take to help eliminate prejudice and discrimination in some specific setting in your community? In your home church?

Chapter 4

Religion That Makes a Difference
James 1:16-27

Nothing is more repulsive to sensitive souls than hypocrisy. Our English word is traceable to the Greek *hypokrisis*, which refers to the playing of a part on the stage. It is "pretending to be what one is not." Young people are especially offended when someone tries to "put them on" and convince them that he is something he is not.

One of the places where hypocrisy is most often found is in religion. A lot of people say they believe in and love Jesus and yet refuse to obey his commandments. He once challenged some people by asking, "Why do you call me, 'Lord, Lord,' and do not do what I say?" (Luke 6:46). He was saying, in effect, that their actions belied their testimony. He was accusing them of hypocrisy.

It is highly probable that you know some people who go to church services on Sunday, sit near the front, and sing loudly; yet these same people live very careless spiritual lives on the other six days of the week. These people are hypocrites. They have a very shallow type of religion which makes no real difference in their lives.

The book of James makes it unmistakably clear that true religion makes a perceptible difference in one's thinking, disposition, language, habits, choice of friends, etc. To live in the kingdom of God is not a matter of inflated claims to spirituality and occasional church attendance. It is the total control of an individual by the will of the Lord Jesus Christ.

In James 1:16-27 the Holy Spirit specifies five areas in which true religion makes a difference in one's life: (1) in his view of God, (2) in his ability to control his temper and

35

tongue, (3) in his heart, (4) in his willingness to obey the Word of God, and (5) in his concern for the needy.

A Difference in Your View of God

First, true religion makes a difference in one's view of God. "Don't be deceived, my dear brothers. Every good and perfect gift is from above, coming down from the Father of the heavenly lights, who does not change like shifting shadows. He chose to give us birth through the word of truth, that we might be a kind of firstfruits of all he created" (James 1:16-18).

In verses 12-15, James had warned his readers against a false view of God which would make him the source of our temptations to evil. The idea that such is the case both degrades God into an evil being and overlooks the great mercies which he constantly pours into our lives. It then degenerates into a fatalistic and whining self-pity which causes one to shirk the responsibilities for his spiritual failures. "Don't be deceived" is James' warning in this regard. If Satan can deceive the Christian by turning his attention from his rich supply of blessings and getting him to brood over his hardships (whether real or imagined), he may be able to create a discontent and frustration adequate to lead him into sin and destruction.

For example, I know a brother who, I am sure, could never have been won to sin by straightforward temptations. But he fell on "hard times," made some serious mistakes, and had to give up his job. He began to wallow in self-pity, gradually disengaged himself from an active involvement in a local church, and finally gave himself over to things he knew were wrong. To blame God for our troubles is dangerous error in one's thinking which can produce terrible consequences.

A baby dies and his parents ask, "Why did God take him from us?" A tragic accident turns a healthy young man into an invalid for the remainder of his life, and he asks, "Why did God do this to me?" A home breaks up and a twelve-year-old girl asks, "Why did God let this happen to my family?" On and on the examples could be given of how people blame God for the problems and temptations that come upon them. No wonder many of them eventually become cynical and bitter toward the Christian faith. They have a wrong view of God.

God is the source of life's *good* things. He does not "set us up" by blessing one day and sending some strong enticement to evil the next. He sends only good things, and he sends them constantly. Solicitation to evil comes from Satan and our own selfish desires, not from God. Trials and stresses of everyday life are not allowed to come for our destruction but for our strengthening.

The nature of God's giving is emphasized in that James calls him the "Father of the heavenly lights" (i.e., sun, moon, and stars) and then contrasts his goodness with the lights he has created. The light of the sun is not constant upon our planet. It varies with the turning of the earth upon its axis. There is bright light at noon which gives way to long shadows in the evening and darkness at night. But God's love and goodness are not occasional and varying in intensity. He is constant and steady with his blessings (cf. 1 John 1:5).

The greatest of all his gifts is salvation. We learn of that gift and how we may receive it through "the word of truth." Then, having been saved in our submission to the gospel, we become "a kind of firstfruits of all he created."

The term "firstfruits" is a common Bible expression which originally referred to the first part of a harvested crop which was given to God. Such an offering was an acknowledgement that the entire crop belonged to God since it had originally come from him as a gift. Using this expressive term of Christians signifies that we belong to God and constitutes a pledge to him of a larger group still to be gathered in unto salvation. God has run our cups over with blessings and intends for us to be a source of blessing to others -- particularly in sharing the gospel. This view of God will make a difference in one's attitude and manner of life. Knowing that God gives only good things, he will not fall prey to Satan's subtle efforts to demoralize him into evil paths. Seeing himself as part of the "firstfruits" of God, he will never be idle in spiritual service.

A Difference in Your Temper and Tongue

Second, true religion makes a difference in one's ability to control his temper and tongue. "My dear brothers, take note of this: Everyone should be quick to listen, slow to speak and slow to become angry, for man's anger does not bring about the righteous life that God desires" (James 1:19-20). Hardly any test of one's religion could be more practical and revealing than this one. Are you able to listen to others? Do you know when to hold your tongue? Can you control your temper?

Being known for a sharp tongue and fiery temper will not make anyone an effective influence for Christ and his church.

Is this to say that we should sit by while people ridicule Christ or the truth? Of course not. But is a public fuss the way to defend truth? Peter wrote under the Spirit's control and urged Christians "to give an answer to everyone who asks you to give the reason for the hope that you have. But do this with gentleness and respect, keeping a clear conscience, so that those who speak maliciously against your good behavior in Christ may be ashamed of their slander" (1 Pet. 3:15b-16). It is ordinarily better to wait for a quieter place and a calmer time and to prayerfully prepare yourself on what you want to say and do about the matter.

Christians fall heir to a great deal of chiding because of some of our beliefs and practices. The fact that a Christian young lady dresses modestly often makes her the object of hurtful remarks and jokes. A Christian young man on the football team who will not go to the victory party and get drunk may take a lot of taunting criticism from his teammates. Insistence on a faith that is obedient and emphasizing biblical authority can get one branded as a legalist.

How do you react to it when you are the object of such criticism? Does it make you mad and tempt you to "tell 'em off"? Or can you dismiss it in good cheer for the time being and wait for a more opportune time to explain your conviction or behavior more carefully? "Blowing your top" and "letting off steam" may be the natural and easy thing for you to do, but it is not the right thing to do.

Whether the conversation or criticism has to do with religion or the weather, be very slow about losing your temper and unleashing your tongue. Even if you win an argument, you may lose a friend or even a soul.

A Difference in Your Heart

Third, true religion makes a difference in one's heart. "Therefore, get rid of all moral filth and the evil that is so prevalent and humbly accept the word planted in you, which can save you" (James 1:21).

When the gospel is preached, there are varied responses to it. For example, when Paul first preached this saving message in Athens "some of them sneered, but others said, 'We want to hear you again on this subject' " (Acts 17:32). Even among those who have received the gospel to the degree that they have become Christians, there are evident differences in the amounts of change wrought in their lives and in the degree of devotion to Christ which has been created. We are forced to wonder why there is such a difference in effect where the gospel is faithfully preached and taught.

The difference does not lie within the gospel itself, for "God does not show favoritism" (Acts 10:35). Thus it must be that the difference in effect relates directly to the individual hearers. The Lord taught as much in the Parable of the Soils (Luke 8:4-15). In this particular parable, the emphasis is on the reception of the gospel by various types of hearts. James, in his epistle on Christian living, treats the same theme by developing the thesis that true religion requires a particular type of heart which is fertile soil for the production of the "fruit of the Spirit" in the lives of Christians.

James 1:21 is about the reception of the Word of God. God's word is able to "save you," but only if you allow it to become "planted" (deeply rooted) in your heart. How does one go about creating a heart within himself that will welcome the gospel?

A heart which will receive the gospel properly and with good effect is identified by the Holy Spirit as having two necessary traits.

First, it must "get rid of all moral filth and the evil that is so prevalent." Some people fail to live the Christian life because they have never accepted the implications of genuine repentance. They have given up most of their sins, but not all of them. They have let some of them carry over from the past and go with them into their "new" life. It cannot be so. The gospel will not have its full effect in producing Christian character and dedication in a person until he discards all the sinful remains of his old life.

Second, he must receive the rebuke and counsel of the Word of God in "meekness." To be meek is to be capable of self-control. Some Christians lack meekness and will not accept the will of God without anger or resentment. They get mad when the Bible rebukes some sin they enjoy and become angry with the teacher who brought the matter to their attention (cf. Gal. 4:16).

So the elements of a good and fruitful heart are *purity* (i.e., genuine remorse over every sin) and *humility* (i.e., the ability to receive rebuke and counsel in the right spirit). An individual whose heart is characterized by these traits will grow daily in his spiritual stature and strength. He will find favor with God and men. He will exert a powerful influence for truth and righteousness.

The Bible consistently regards the heart as the key to character (cf. Prov. 4:23; Matt. 15:19). In its unregenerated state, the heart is corrupt. Salvation is therefore pictured as an operation in which a man's heart is changed (cf. Rom. 2:29). What about your heart? Has it really been changed since you became a Christian? Or are you still holding onto some of your old vices and resisting the teachings of the Word of God?

Whether an individual receives the implanted word and has the desired effect produced in his life depends entirely on him. A hypocrite will be content to go through the motions of Christianity without undergoing a total transformation of his being. But one who practices true religion will yield altogether to the will of God in being changed "from the inside out" (i.e., from his heart to his behavior). Which type of person have you been?

A Difference in Your Willingness to Obey

Fourth, true religion makes a difference in one's willingness to submit to authority and obey commands. "Do not merely listen to the word, and so deceive yourselves. Do what it says. Anyone who listens to the word but does not do what it says is like a man who looks at his face in a mirror and, after looking at himself, goes away and immediately forgets what he looks like. But the man who looks intently into the perfect law that gives freedom, and continues to do this, not forgetting what he has heard, but doing it -- he will be blessed in what he does" (James 1:22-25).

The truths of the gospel must be translated into concrete actions. Attending a worship service, listening to a sermon, and giving brief attention to some important truth

41

are of no value if a difference is not made in one's actual behavior as a result. Some people have evidently convinced themselves that the contemplation of some good thing is the same as being good. Sometimes people leave an auditorium and tell the preacher, "That sermon really hit me!" Perhaps the reply to that comment should be, "Well, what are you going to do about it?" Listening to the painful truth is not a whipping which squares your account with God; it is a form of prodding to get you to do something once you have left the assembly.

James declares that those Christians who are content with a hearing-but-not-doing religion are deceiving themselves. He compares them to a man who sees a reflection of his dirty face and uncombed hair in the mirror but does nothing about it. When a person looks into the mirror of God's Word, he sees himself both as he really is and as he ought to be. But the careless and indifferent hearer makes no effort to bridge the gap between the two. The hearing has been for nothing insofar as he is concerned. The "blessed" (happy) man is the Christian who hears with patience and then acts on what he has learned.

Verse 25 speaks of the man who "looks intently into the perfect law." This expression literally refers to one who stoops down to take a close look at himself and seriously attempts to change the image he has seen reflected. This is the happy man. The man who fights the Word of God is wretched and miserable as he struggles with a guilty conscience. The one who yields to God in obedience has a clear conscience and receives the blessings of God in his dedicated life.

This section of James reminds one of the words of Jesus in the Sermon on the Mount: "Therefore everyone who hears these words of mine and puts them into practice is like a wise man who built his house on the rock. The rain came down, the streams rose, and the winds blew and beat against that house; yet it did not fall, because it had its foundation on the rock. But everyone who hears these words of mine and does not put them into practice is like a foolish man who built his house on sand. The rain came down, the streams rose, and the winds blew and beat against that house, and it fell with a great crash" (Matt. 7:24-27).

The hypocrite listens, nods approvingly, and affirms his agreement with the truth. He then goes on his way to behave precisely as *he* pleases -- even if in doing so he must defy the truth he has just heard. The individual practicing true religion examines his life in light of the truth he hears and reorders his thinking and behavior accordingly. Which type of hearer are you?

A Difference in Your Concern for the Needy

Fifth, true religion makes a difference in one's degree of sincere concern for and actions on behalf of the needy. "If anyone considers himself religious and yet does not keep a tight rein on his tongue, he deceives himself and his religion is worthless. Religion that God our Father accepts as pure and faultless is this: to look after orphans and widows in their distress and to keep oneself from being polluted by the world" (James 1:26-27). After reemphasizing the evils of an unrestrained tongue (cf. v. 19), James stresses the fact that "pure and faultless" religion demands that Christians manifest an active regard for people with special needs.

Heaven has always been solicitous for the needy. Orphans and widows seem to have been particular objects of this divine concern. "A father to the fatherless, a defender of widows, is God in his holy dwelling" (Psa. 68:5). With God's concern for these people being so great, surely we would expect him to require his people to be observant to their welfare. So we are required to "look after" them in the epistle of James. And this implies more than making a

43

social call or observing the situation; it refers to relieving their needs.

For a child of God to shut his heart to the plight of distressed people around him would make his religion vain. It would make him a hypocrite.

We must show compassion to all men. "Therefore, as God's chosen people, holy and dearly loved, clothe yourselves with compassion, kindness, humility, gentleness and patience" (Col. 3:12). And especially we must show concern for our brethren. "Therefore, as we have opportunity, let us do good to all people, especially to those who belong to the family of believers" (Gal. 6:10). "If anyone has material possessions and sees his brother in need but has no pity on him, how can the love of God be in him?" (1 John 3:17).

One way we can help the hurting and needy is to give money -- either individually or through the treasury of the local congregation -- to those who are in need. But have we turned this type of good work into a salve for our consciences and an excuse to keep from "getting our hands dirty" in the business of caring for the needy?

Are there widows or needy families in your community or congregation that you could help directly? Is there some elderly person or couple whose yard work could be done by young people in the church? Are there poor, handicapped, or lonely people you know who tend to be left on the sidelines of life?

The fact that Jesus loved people and met their needs gained a favorable hearing for the message he preached. If we were more like him, we would gain a more favorable hearing for his gospel when we try to tell it to others.

Conclusion

One of the great sins of ancient Israel was the reducing of their religion to ritual and ceremony. They neglected the practical matters of their religion and simply went through its external forms.

Micah was especially severe in denouncing this shallow and hypocritical substitute for true religion. "With what shall I come before the Lord and bow down before the exalted God? Shall I come before him with burnt offerings, with calves a year old? Will the Lord be pleased with thousands of rams, with ten thousand rivers of oil? Shall I offer my firstborn for my transgression, the fruit of my body for the sin of my soul? He has showed you, O man, what is good. And what does the Lord require of you? To act justly and to love mercy and to walk humbly with your God" (Mic. 6:6-8).

God's attitude has not changed. He still hates hypocrisy. Our outward expressions of religion such as public worship and prayer are necessary. But we are foolish to think that our heavenly Father wants nothing more. He expects us to live our faith.

What is Christian living all about? It is correct doctrine, but it is more. It is translating correct doctrine into correct behavior. If your religion is mere form which has made no real difference in your life, you are playing at the serious matter of Christianity and need to take the message of James to heart.

Memorize: Matthew 7:24-27

TAKE THOUGHT

1. Why is it such a dangerous thing for one to blame God for his troubles? Can you cite an example of how such an attitude has contributed to someone's spiritual decline? Discuss the importance of our being observant to people who are going through great trials.

2. What are some of the situations which provoke you most? Are you prone to lose your temper under these circumstances? What might you say? What are you doing to bring temper and tongue under control?

3. Discuss the different ways people react to the Word of God. What is your customary reaction to learning something which makes a demand on you?

4. In what way is a man a hypocrite to hear the Word of God without obeying it? Discuss obedience as it relates to having a clear conscience (cf. 1 Pet. 3:21).

5. What is involved in the command to "look after orphans and widows in their distress" in James 1:27?

TAKE ACTION

1. Conduct a panel discussion in class on the responsibility of the church in teaching the lost about Christ. Suggest some specific things that class members can do to reach their friends and neighbors.

2. Appoint someone from the class to contact an elder or the chairman of the benevolence committee to learn of someone (e.g., widow, invalid, etc.) whom the members of this class can "adopt" and to whom you can give attention and regular help (e.g., visits, shopping, house cleaning, etc.).

3. Take a piece of paper and write down (for your exclusive viewing and use) the things which threaten most to "pollute" you with worldly things. Decide what you can do by way of a defense against these things. If some of them are already getting you down, don't be ashamed to confess it to someone you trust and ask for help in dealing with them.

Chapter 5

Faith That Saves
James 2:14-26

One of the great and abiding disputes among religious people has been over the relationship between faith and works. And no single passage of Scripture bearing on the subject has been more of a battleground in the controversy than James 2:14-26. It was this passage which so seriously challenged Martin Luther's theory of salvation by faith alone that he designated the entire epistle of James "an epistle of straw" and left it out of his canon of New Testament books.

Martin Luther and several other critics of this epistle contend that James contradicts Paul on the relative merit of faith and deeds. Modern religious teachers certainly contradict each other on the subject.

Let us examine this text very closely and then compare James' teaching with that of Paul and other New Testament writers on this important biblical theme.

Faith Without Deeds Is Dead

James opens with the clear affirmation that faith apart from action is dead. "What good is it, my brothers, if a man claims to have faith but has no deeds? Can such faith save him: Suppose a brother or sister is without clothes and daily food. If one of you says to him, 'Go, I wish you well; keep warm and well fed,' but does nothing about his physical needs, what good is it? In the same way, faith by itself, if it is not accompanied by action, is dead" (James 2:14-17).

James considers the possibility of a claim to faith and how to validate it. Is it enough for one to assert his faith? Or must there be the evidence of obedience to prove that assertion? One is reminded of these words from Jesus: "Not everyone who says to me, 'Lord, Lord,' will enter the

47

kingdom of heaven, but only he who does the will of my Father who is in heaven" (Matt. 7:21). Profession is meaningless without performance.

A Spirit-guided illustration of this truth concerns a brother who is destitute and hungry. One sees this brother's needs and says, "Good luck to you!" How much good has he done the man? Should he not have backed up his profession of good will with some tangible relief? James is here underscoring again the theme of this whole epistle -- Christianity must be practical in order to be real. Actions are necessary to validate one's faith.

The Bible makes a clear distinction between "dead" faith and "living" faith.

Dead faith is faith that understands, gives assent to facts, but does not act based on the information received. That kind of faith is worthless. It corresponds to a man who is terribly ill saying, "Yes, I believe in my doctor. He is an excellent physician, and I believe that he is able to prescribe treatment which will restore my health." Then the man refuses to take the medicine which the doctor prescribes. What kind of faith does he have in his physician? In spite of the fact that he has claimed to have unbounded confidence in the man, he belies his claim by his actions. If he really believes in his doctor, he would take the medication which was prescribed.

Living faith is that faith which trusts enough to follow carefully whatever instructions may be given. Dead faith is without value; only living faith avails. No man can legitimately say that he believes in Jesus Christ if he is unwilling to do the things Christ has commanded about salvation and eternal life. Saying "Lord, Lord" will not do as a substitute for actually doing the Father's will.

James moves next to anticipate a possible objection. Someone might say, "But different men may choose to exhibit their religion in different ways -- one by faith and another by deeds." He challenges anyone who would make

48

so naive a statement to show his faith apart from the fruit it produces in his life. "But someone will say, 'You have faith; I have deeds.' Show me your faith without deeds, and I will show you my faith by what I do. You believe that there is one God. Good. Even the demons believe that -- and shudder. You foolish man, do you want evidence that faith without deeds is useless?" (James 2:18-20).

There is no proof that a man has faith at all unless some fruit is borne of it in his life. If one claims to have faith in God and his Word and yet lives as a liar, thief, and reprobate, he proves that his faith is not real. But if one claims to have faith and then proceeds to develop Christian character by his obedience to the Word of God, he is proving the truthfulness of the claim he has made.

Even the demons believe in the one true God; but they are lost and doomed forever because they did not, in their previous existence as angels (cf. 2 Pet. 2:4), keep God's commandments. The same sad fate will befall many human beings who profess faith and refuse to be obedient to the will of God as revealed in Scripture.

True Faith Exemplified

Two familiar and clear examples of faith that saves are set forth in the text.

First, consider the case of Abraham. "Was not our ancestor Abraham considered righteous for what he did when he offered his son Isaac on the altar? You see that his faith and his actions were working together, and his faith was made complete by what he did. And the scripture was fulfilled that says, 'Abraham believed God, and it was credited to him as righteousness,' and he was called God's friend. You see that a person is justified by what he does and not by faith alone" (James 2:21-24).

The Jewish Christians who first read this epistle would be familiar with the fact that Abraham was the "father of the faithful" or the "father of those who believe." Yet James reminds his readers that Abraham was not justified before God until he had obeyed the requirement to give Isaac as a sacrifice. And the scripture which says "Abraham believed God" was not fulfilled until after he had obeyed the Lord in this regard (cf. Gen. 22:1-19; Heb. 11:17-19). If it was obedient faith that justified Abraham, will anything less justify us?

Second, consider the case of Rahab. "In the same way, was not even Rahab the prostitute considered righteous for what she did when she gave lodging to the spies and sent them off in a different direction?" (James 2:25). This example of faith takes the reader back to the time of Israel's entry into the Promised Land, Canaan. Joshua sent spies into Jericho to bring back a report concerning that city. The faith of Rahab that these men were from God would have been in vain if she had not acted on her conviction. She did act by hiding the men and later sending them out safely to rejoin the Israelites. Shortly thereafter, when her home city of Jericho was given to God's people in a terrible battle, Rahab and her family were spared destruction because of her faith (cf. Josh. 2:1-24). Her faith saved her because her faith acted.

The only legitimate conclusion to be drawn from these examples is this: *One is saved by his faith when that faith leads him to do what God has directed. Faith that refuses to obey is not saving faith.* One does not truly believe God if he is not willing to follow God's directions. One would be as foolish to say that he had a firm faith in God while refusing to obey the commands God has given about salvation from alien sins and Christian living as to say that he had confidence in his doctor while refusing to take the medicine he had prescribed.

As James expressed it, "As the body without the spirit is dead, so faith without deeds is dead" (James 2:26).

The Nature of Faith

The very nature of faith requires the believer to be active in his or her response to God. From Hebrews 11:1 comes a biblical description of faith: "Now faith is being sure of what we hope for and certain of what we do not see." Faith is knowledge which comes through the acceptance of reliable testimony. We could never have discovered heaven by accident. Someone had to inform us of its existence, desirability, and availability. Our acceptance of this information through another's credible testimony is faith. We could never have discovered God's will for our salvation by our own feeble investigations. This had to be revealed to us. Our confidence in the plan of salvation set forth in Scripture is faith. The assurance and conviction which comes from accepting trustworthy testimony on any matter is faith.

But one's assurance of the existence of heaven and his conviction that the Bible points the way to that wonderful place will not allow him to be passive. He will begin to seek God actively and to demonstrate his eager desire for God's eternal fellowship by bringing his heart and life into conformity with the divine will.

Indeed, according to Hebrews 11:6, faith enables us to please God because it causes us to seek him according to his revealed will. "And without faith it is impossible to please God, because anyone who comes to him must believe that he exists and that he rewards those who earnestly seek him." The whole of one's life on earth will be only as successful as his faith is strong, for faith is the foundation for a life that is actually lived according to the righteous pattern set before mankind in the Bible.

The Alleged Contradiction

What shall we make of the contradiction that some say exists between the teaching of James and Paul on this

51

subject? The charge stems from comparing these two statements: "For we maintain that a man is justified by faith apart from observing the law" (Rom. 3:28). "You see that a person is justified by what he does and not by faith alone" (James 2:24). At first glance, one may be convinced that these two passages are contradictory.

If one understands that these two men are writing to different audiences and dealing with altogether different matters, the suspicion of contradiction vanishes.

Paul was writing to refute certain false teachers who taught that salvation depended on doing good works and accumulating merit for them. For some, those meritorious deeds would have been the works of the Law of Moses. Thus they would have attempted to bind circumcision, sabbath-keeping, and certain other Old Testament ordinances on New Testament Christians. Paul asserted that the works of the Law have nothing to do with the salvation of men under the authority of Christ. More than that, no amount of rule-keeping under any system -- pagan, Jewish, or Christian -- can remedy a sinner's relationship with God.

On the other hand, James was writing to refute the false notion that faith -- understood as inner conviction and personal confidence -- was all that mattered in religion. He taught that inner conviction has to show itself in the outward deeds of the individual. Thus it is that the "contradiction" in these two passages is only imagined rather than real. Paul and James were discussing two different types of works.

Just as surely as there are two types of faith discussed in the New Testament (i.e., dead faith and living faith), so are two types of works discussed (i.e., deeds of meritorious good works and deeds of submissive, non-meritorious obedience to Christ).

A close examination of the teaching of Paul will show that he taught that a man is saved by faith if and only if that faith is genuine enough to lead him to respond to the gospel in obedience. He wrote: "For in Christ Jesus neither circumcision nor uncircumcision has any value. The only thing that counts is faith expressing itself through love" (Gal. 5:6).

Paul and James are in perfect harmony in their teaching on this matter. Both make it clear that faith and obedience are not in opposition to each other. They are two sides of the same coin in God's plan for the salvation of man. Man must believe in God and take him at his word. Based on that faith, he must obey the commands that God has given. At the end of all he has done, however, he gives God praise for saving him by grace; he makes no claim to be saved by his own good deeds.

In a nutshell, the biblical tension is never between faith and action. It is between faith and merit as the ground of one's salvation.

The faith that saves is illustrated in the eleventh chapter of Hebrews. This great chapter speaks of many heroes of biblical history who were saved by their faith -- Abraham, Noah, Enoch, and many others. "By faith Abel offered God a better sacrifice than Cain did. . . . By faith Noah, when warned about things not yet seen, in holy fear built an ark to save his family. . . . By faith Abraham, when called to go to a place he would later receive as his inheritance, obeyed and went, even though he did not know where he was going" (Heb. 11:4, 7, 8).

Notice in each of these instances that the individual is said to have obeyed some command of God *by faith*. Faith did not cause these men to shrink from action. Faith was the basis of their action. So must faith be the basis for our obedience to God in order for faith to save us. In none of these cases did the people save themselves or earn their salvation. In them all, God saved the people by his grace through their trust in him -- a trust they showed when they responded to him in submissive compliance with his will.

Significance of Deeds to Salvation

As James used the word in his epistle, "deeds" refers to one's acts of obedience to the commandments of God. One cannot be saved without such a demonstration of his faith. To be sure, he cannot earn or merit his salvation by piling up good deeds and boasting about them. But neither can he be saved in rebellion against the Father in heaven. There is no cause for pride or boasting in these acts of obedience. They are the deeds of a humble and submissive person who is seeking only to do the will of God as that will has been revealed in Scripture.

To the non-Christian, this means that he cannot afford to fall prey to the false denominational doctrine of salvation by faith alone. One cannot be saved from his sins by simply "trusting Christ as your personal Savior and receiving him into your heart." This doctrine dates back to a wrong turn in Reformation theology and contradicts the clear teaching of James 2:24 and other New Testament passages. Inquiring sinners of the first century were not told, "Only believe and do nothing more!" They were commanded, "Repent and be baptized, every one of you, in the name of Jesus Christ for the forgiveness of your sins. And you will receive the gift of the Holy Spirit" (Acts 2:38).

To the Christian, this means that his life will have to bear fruit daily if he is to demonstrate his new state in the Lord and avoid falling away. His faith must prompt him to faithfulness in the Lord's service -- Bible study, prayer, regular worship, teaching the lost of salvation, etc. Otherwise his faith is dead and utterly without value.

Conclusion

It is imperative that we understand that God is not calling us to choose between faith and deeds as alternative ways to salvation. He is calling us to salvation by the one and only path which leads to eternal life -- the path of faith which shows itself in appropriate deeds.

What is Christian living all about? It is the exhibition of one's faith in his willing obedience to God's will for his life. It is backing up one's profession with performance. It is nurturing one's faith to life through deeds rather than stifling it to death through inactivity. What type of faith do you have?

Memorize: Hebrews 11:6

TAKE THOUGHT

1. Do James and Paul teach different things about faith? What do they teach about works in relation to faith?

2. Discuss James' illustration of faith without deeds (2:14-17). Have you ever seen anything comparable to this? Have you ever been guilty of anything like it?

3. Discuss the relationship between faith and knowledge. Are the two opposed to each other? Is faith unrelated to reason, logic, and proof? Or is faith a special means of gaining knowledge?

4. The Bible teaches there are two types of faith. Discuss and illustrate each.

5. The Bible also teaches there are two types of works. Discuss and illustrate each. Notice John 6:29 in connection with questions 4 and 5.

TAKE ACTION

1. Do some research into the life of Martin Luther in order to understand why he came to his view of salvation of faith alone. Notice the strong emphasis in his earlier life on meritorious deeds. Was it totally unpredictable that he should have swung from one extreme to another?

2. Secure some of the creed books or confessions of major Protestant bodies in America. What is their doctrine of salvation? How does this doctrine compare with James' teaching?

3. What are some things you are saying but not doing in your Christian life? How will you take action immediately to translate your faith into action?

Chapter 6

Taming the Tongue
James 3:1-12; 4:11-12; 5:12

Some people carry instruments of life and death with them as a matter of routine requirement. For example, policemen wear loaded guns and physicians carry powerful drugs. People with that sort of power over others have to feel a keen sense of responsibility. Certainly such powerful instruments should never be put into the hands of a foolish, immature, or irresponsible person.

The Bible teaches: "The tongue has the power of life and death" (Prov. 18:21).

The tongue is capable of *great good*. "The tongue that brings healing is a tree of life. . . . and how good is a timely word!" (Prov. 15:4, 23). It is also capable of *great harm*. Therefore David resolved, "I will watch my ways and keep my tongue from sin; I will put a muzzle on my mouth as long as the wicked are in my presence" (Psa. 39:1).

Every one of us carries and wields this powerful instrument every day. A thoughtful and kind tongue can encourage the weak and exhort the wayward. It can give life. A foolish or malicious tongue can destroy personalities and reputations. It can kill. Would that we all felt as keen a sense of responsibility for the use of our tongues as the policeman does for the use of his gun or the physician for the use of his powerful medications.

No wiser counsel about the tongue and its proper use can be found than the inspired counsel given by James in his epistle.

The Danger of an Uncontrolled Tongue

The third chapter of James opens with a specific warning to Christian teachers and to those who aspire to such

57

work. "Not many of you should presume to be teachers, my brothers, because you know that we who teach will be judged more strictly" (James 3:1). This statement was not intended to discourage teachers or to cause Christians to waste their opportunities to teach. Rather it was intended to exhort teachers to do their work out of a pure motivation and with careful restraint over their tongues.

The role of teacher was indispensable and highly respected in the early church. Thus some were tempted to become teachers out of a love for preeminence among their brethren. Furthermore, there was the potential harm a teacher could do with his tongue in the exercise of his office. For one thing, he could cause men to be condemned by teaching them falsehoods (cf. 2 Thess. 2:10-12). For another, he could be tempted to win personal loyalties to himself by flattery and guile (cf. Rom. 16:18). Again, he could be guilty of distracting from Christ by a display of worldly wisdom in his teaching (cf. 1 Cor. 2:1).

Because of dangers such as these, one must be very careful about his motives and manner as a teacher. Teachers will be judged by a stricter standard than other Christians -- both by men in this life and by God in the final Judgment.

Turning from this specific warning to teachers, verses 2-5a constitute a more general warning to all Christians about the need for controlling the tongue. "We all stumble in many ways. If anyone is never at fault in what he says, he is a perfect man, able to keep his whole body in check. When we put bits into the mouths of horses to make them obey us, we can turn the whole animal. Or take ships as an example. Although they are so large and are driven by strong winds, they are steered by a very small rudder wherever the pilot wants to go. Likewise the tongue is a small part of the body, but it makes great boasts."

Don't miss the boldness of this passage. It asserts that a man who can control his tongue -- the most unruly part of his whole body -- can control his entire being.

The ability of one's tongue to control his very life and eternal destiny is seen in its comparison to bits in a horse's mouth and a ship's rudder. The tongue really is this powerful. So if you want your life to turn out right, you must do something about bringing your tongue under control. You must bring it, along with every other part of your being, under subjection to the will of God (cf. Rom. 6:12-13).

The absolute necessity of having control over one's tongue is emphasized when he sees the danger and harm of a tongue out of control. Such an untamed tongue is "a fire." "Consider what a great forest is set on fire by a small spark. The tongue also is a fire, a world of evil among the parts of the body. It corrupts the whole person, sets the whole course of his life on fire, and is itself set on fire by hell" (James 3:5b-6). It is also a "restless evil" and is "full of deadly poison." "All kinds of animals, birds, reptiles and creatures of the sea are being tamed and have been tamed by man, but no man can tame the tongue. It is a restless evil, full of deadly poison" (James 3:7-8).

Nothing is more inconsistent with true religion than for a Christian to use his tongue to sing praise to God on Sunday and to curse his neighbor or co-worker on other days of the week. It is absurd. But still it happens all too often. "With the tongue we praise our Lord and Father, and with it we curse men, who have been made in God's likeness. Out of the same mouth come praise and cursing. My brothers, this should not be. Can both fresh water and salt water flow from the same spring? My brothers, can a fig tree bear olives, or a grapevine bear figs? Neither can a salt spring produce fresh water" (James 3:9-12).

Speaking Evil of Another

One of the specific sins of an uncontrolled tongue which James discusses in this epistle is unjust and evil judgment of someone else. "Brothers, do not slander one another. Anyone who speaks against his brother or judges him speaks against the law and judges it. When you judge the law, you are not keeping it, but sitting in judgment on it. There is only one Lawgiver and Judge, the one who is able to save and destroy. But you -- who are you to judge your neighbor?" (James 4:11-12).

Now, this passage must not be misunderstood and misused. It *does not* forbid all kinds of judging. For example, it does not forbid the opposition of a false teacher, for this is commanded of us in 1 John 4:1. It does not forbid a congregation to judge sin in its midst and to take action against those involved, for 1 Corinthians 5:3 and 12 obviously teach that a congregation must do this. The correct interpretation of this matter of judging was given by Jesus in these words: "Stop judging by mere appearances and make a right judgment" (John 7:24). The Christian *must judge* right and wrong based on the Word of God. But he *must not judge* his fellows out of hatred, pride, or some other false motive.

C. Leslie Mitton makes these helpful comments on this passage:

> The Greek word here translated "SPEAK EVIL AGAINST" (*katalaleo*) means literally "to talk somebody down," "to disparage." It means speaking of others in a way calculated to lower them in other people's estimation, and speaking of them in their absence, when they have no opportunity to defend themselves or correct untrue statements. That is why in the older translations this word was often translated "backbite," with its suggestion of a hurtful injury inflicted on a man behind his back. (*The Epistle of James*, p. 164.)

Obviously it is wrong to tell a lie about another person or to make a willful false accusation against him. Lying is of the devil (John 8:44), and a "lying tongue" is one of the things God hates (cf. Prov. 6:16-19). Beyond this obvious fact, the pointless telling of a real fault in another's life is also sinful. It is not enough to say, "But I know this to be the truth about John Doe and what he did." To tell of a real fault in another is unjustified unless it is for his own good or for the protection of some innocent party. Any other basis for such a revelation would turn it into mere gossip or slander. Rotary International has a "Four-Way Test" which the Christian would do well to apply to his speech: (1) Is it the truth? (2) Is it fair to all concerned? (3) Will it bring good will and better friendship? (4) Will it be beneficial to all concerned?

It is so easy to have keen eyes for the failings of others while being blind to one's own failings. "Why do you look at the speck of sawdust in your brother's eye and pay no attention to the plank in your own eye?" asked the Lord (Matt. 7:3). Let any person be praised in a conversation and there is almost always some hateful soul present who cannot resist the temptation to "balance the scales" by adding a negative comment. It is an unlovely spirit in anyone. Any unskilled person can tear down a church, a family, or a person. Only a skilled workman can build up others by the right use of his tongue.

Shall we constantly judge, criticize, and find fault in the lives of good people who are sincerely trying to do the Lord's will and who would love to be our friends? Shall we not rather try to overcome a critical spirit toward others by looking for ways to compliment and encourage them?

There is so much bad in the best of us,
And so much good in the worst of us,
That it hardly behooves any of us,
To talk about the rest of us.

As James pointed out, only God has the right to be a "lawgiver and judge." We must respect his judgments but resist the temptation to pass our own capricious judgments. To do otherwise is to sin dreadfully with our tongues.

Foolish Oaths

Another sin frequently committed by an uncontrolled tongue is specified in James 5:12. "Above all, my brothers, do not swear -- not by heaven or by earth or by anything else. Let your 'Yes,' be yes, and your 'No,' no, or you will be condemned."

Some have mistakenly taken James' prohibition of oath-taking to mean that a Christian could not testify "under oath" in a legal proceeding. But that the prohibition of legitimate oaths is not forbidden here is evident in that (1) Christ answered to an oath in Matthew 26:63-64, (2) Paul took oaths on such occasions as 2 Corinthians 1:23 and Galatians 1:20, and (3) the taking of oaths is mentioned without rebuke in Hebrews 6:16. Christians may take spiritual oaths of commitment to the Lord or take an oath in a courtroom; but in the ordinary affairs of life we are to be persons of unquestioned honor and truthfulness and avoid unnecessary and foolish oaths such as had become common in James' day.

Men of the first-century world had made a mockery of oath-taking by coming to distinguish between binding and non-binding oaths. They had come to regard the truth so lightly that they used oaths altogether too freely. James rebuked such conduct and placed Christians under the obligation to speak truthfully under all circumstances without the necessity of taking oaths.

A child of God should never be compelled to ask another Christian to confirm his statement with an oath. And no Christian should be so careless and hypocritical in his speech as to feel compelled to certify certain statements with an oath. To say that "God is my witness . . ." or "Goodness knows that . . ." is unworthy of a child of the living God. "Therefore each of you must put off falsehood and speak truthfully to his neighbor, for we are all members of one body" (Eph. 4:25).

Other Improper Uses of the Tongue

In connection with James' exhortations respecting the taming of the tongue, several other instances of its improper use come to mind.

Profanity is certainly the exercise of an uncontrolled tongue. The name of God is sacred and is never to be used with irreverence or disrespect. "You shall not misuse the name of the Lord your God, for the Lord will not hold anyone guiltless who misuses his name" (Ex. 20:7; cf. Psa. 111:9; Neh. 9:5). Profanity is not a mark of maturity but is rather a reflection upon one's intelligence. One ought to be able to express his feelings without having to resort to the sinful use of God's holy name.

In spite of the fact that most Christians would never think of using profanity forthrightly, many nevertheless use occasional bywords or euphemisms which come dangerously close -- and perhaps even cross the line -- to dishonoring the name of God. Surely this is done out of ignorance and not out of a conscious desire to take the name of God improperly.

For example, it is not uncommon to hear someone say, "Lord, have mercy!" Whether the news heard is good or bad, this expression seems to be thought appropriate to express surprise or shock. But to utter such an expression is to use the name of the Lord in a vain and careless manner.

The words "gosh" or "golly" are euphemisms for the name of God. "Gee" or "gee whiz" is a euphemism for the name of Jesus. *Webster's Third New International Dictionary* so defines these words. And lest someone object that people who use these words do not intend them as substitutes for the name of God, the fact nevertheless remains that the words have a defined meaning just as every other word in the English language. One might just as reasonably say that he is going to use the word "house" to mean something other than its defined meaning as to say that he is going to use these euphemisms without regard to their definitions.

And what about such expressions as "goodness gracious" or "for goodness sake"? Webster says such expressions originally referred to the goodness of God. Thus, to say the least, they place one on dangerous ground relative to the sacred versus the profane use of the divine name. And many who would be horrified at the word "hell" used as an oath nevertheless use "my heavens" or "for heaven's sake" in their conversations. This in spite of the fact that Jesus said, "And he who swears by heaven swears by God's throne and by the one who sits on it" (Matt. 23:22).

The child of God must take care to keep his tongue free from all profanity -- whether obvious or veiled in nature. Each Christian should give thought to the words and expressions just mentioned and examine his own speech habits in light of them. "Simply let your 'Yes' be 'Yes,' and your 'No,' 'No'; anything beyond this comes from the evil one" (Matt. 5:37).

Hypocrisy with one's tongue is also a danger facing the Christian. One may sing "Blest be the tie that binds our hearts in Christian love" and then act in a terribly unloving manner toward his brother. He may sing "Take time to be holy" and then never read his Bible or pray. He may sing "My Jesus, I love thee" and then neglect assembling with the church for two or three weeks. This is hypocrisy in that an individual professes one thing and practices another. And the Lord's most scathing rebukes were directed toward hypocrites (cf. Matt. 23).

Complaining is another fruit of an uncontrolled tongue. Even after God had delivered Israel from Egypt by his wondrous power and had provided for their needs in the wilderness by repeated miracles, these thankless people complained about their lot. God's displeasure with their attitude was evident when he said, "How long will this wicked community grumble against me? I have heard the complaints of these grumbling Israelites" (Num. 14:27).

If God could be provoked to anger by ancient Israel and their complainings, how must he regard ours? We are the richest, yet most dissatisfied, generation in the history of the world.

Some Virtuous Uses of the Tongue

A final consideration with respect to the use of the tongue is learning how to use it constructively. It is not enough to restrain one's tongue from dispensing death. He must learn how to use it to give life. Here are but a few general suggestions on this point.

The Christian should use his tongue for *prayer*. Paul exhorts Christians to "pray continually" (1 Thess. 5:17). Of all the possible good uses to which one could put his tongue, what could be more spiritually profitable than this? Pray about personal problems and special temptations. Pray for the sick. Pray for people who need salvation. Pray for weak and wayward brethren. Pray, pray, pray.

The Christian should use his tongue for *praise* and *thanksgiving*. He should "continually offer to God a sacrifice of praise -- the fruit of lips that confess his name" (Heb. 13:15). It is beneath a Christian to attribute his good fortune to fate or chance circumstance. Every good gift is from God, and he is to be praised and thanked for his goodness (James 1:17). His children must be quick to confess him and acknowledge him before men.

In particular, a Christian should be faithful in his participation in the public praise of God through *worship*. He should be eager to assemble with his brethren and to join with them in using his tongue for the praise of God in song. "Speak to one another with psalms, hymns and spiritual songs. Sing and make music in your heart to the Lord, always giving thanks to God the Father for everything, in the name of our Lord Jesus Christ" (Eph. 5:19-20).

The Christian should use his tongue to *instruct people in the gospel* and to exhort them to salvation. So long as there is just one unsaved person in his acquaintance, the Christian's work is not finished. It is his responsibility to plead with people to believe and obey the gospel. He must try to restore his erring brethren. If a child of God really believes the gospel is able to save men from the terrors of eternal hell and secure them a heavenly inheritance, he will be searching constantly for opportunities to teach it.

A Christian should use his tongue to *encourage* people who are experiencing great difficulties. Crises come to people in various ways -- personal failure and disgrace, sickness, injury, bereavement, family problems. These people need someone to stand near them and to offer encouragement and aid. "But I don't have all the answers. What can I tell these people?" asks someone. Here are a few general suggestions that will be helpful to anyone who is trying to help a despondent person.

First, remind him of his friends who love him, who will pray for him, and who will help him. Second, speak to him of God's love and concern. Remind him that even if everyone else should fail him, God's love abides (cf. Rom. 8:38-39). Third, express confidence in his ability to bear his trial. Especially should his attention be called to the fact that God has promised never to let any trial come to us but that we will be able to bear it (cf. 1 Cor. 10:13). Fourth, help him look beyond the problems of the moment to the time when things will be better (cf. Rom. 8:28). As Solomon wrote in the long ago: "A word aptly spoken is like apples of gold in settings of silver" (Prov. 25:11).

Conclusion

It will help one to control his tongue if he realizes that he is not through with his words once they have been spoken. He will meet them again in the Judgment. "But I tell you that men will have to give account on the day of judgment for every careless word they have spoken. For by your words you will be acquitted, and by your words you will be condemned" (Matt. 12:36-37).

What is Christian living all about? It is the bringing of one's total being under the control of God. And at no point will one find this challenge greater or more rewarding than regarding the bridling of an unruly tongue.

Memorize: Psalm 39:1

TAKE THOUGHT

1. Discuss James' assertion that the tongue has direct influence over one's whole life. Has your tongue ever gotten you into a situation where everything you were doing stemmed from a rash statement, lie, or other wrong use of the tongue? What commitment of your whole life did you make when you confessed Christ at your baptism?

2. Why do people use profanity? How can one purify his speech if he has already become accustomed to foul language?

3. What motives underlie faultfinding and unjust judging? How do people justify this evil use of the tongue?

4. Discuss James 5:12 in detail. Does this forbid Christians being "sworn in" at a legal proceeding? What does it forbid?

5. What positive uses can be made of the tongue?

TAKE ACTION

1. Ask the preacher at your congregation to visit your class and tell you something of the sense of responsibility he feels in the use of his tongue as a teacher. Does this make you feel more sympathetic toward his work?

2. Secure a dictionary of slang from a public library. Check its definitions for some of the euphemisms mentioned in this chapter. List some of the slang words you use commonly and look them up to see their origin and meaning. Do you need to "pull some weeds" out of your vocabulary?

3. Memorize the "Four-Way Test" of Rotary International.

Chapter 7

Wise Up!
James 3:13-18

We are living at a time when human knowledge is expanding at a phenomenal pace. Scientific discovery has already opened many doors to mankind, yet it is estimated that fully 90 percent of all the scientists who have ever lived are alive today. What wondrous things you will likely see in your lifetime. What frightening things you will surely see as well.

It is estimated that the world's body of knowledge doubles every ten years. So much data is now available to humankind that some researchers spend their entire lifetimes trying to discover more effective methods of recording and storing all this information.

The accumulation of so much information has caused men to believe they are terribly wise. This feeling has, in turn, led to arrogance and pride. It has set off international arms races, internal jealousies and conflicts in every "civilized" nation of the world, and personal discontent among individuals. It has caused men to feel that they no longer need God and to serve the created world rather than its Creator. As Paul expressed it, men's "thinking became futile and their foolish hearts were darkened. Although they claimed to be wise, they became fools..." (Rom. 1:21b-22).

A fact that most of us seem not to comprehend is that knowledge and wisdom are not the same. Knowledge is the accumulation of facts; wisdom is the ability to use those facts responsibly. A major problem of our day is that man's knowledge has surpassed his wisdom. We have information, weapons, and technology that we are not handling constructively. Someone needs to tell our world to "Wise up!"

Maybe you know someone that needs to be told to "wise up" in his or her personal behavior. Perhaps it is someone in your office who does good work, is good looking, and has nice clothes but who is rude, foul-mouthed, and generally obnoxious to everyone. Or maybe there are some habits and attitudes which you have that need changing. You may need to "wise up" about certain things.

James and Wisdom

This concern with wisdom is a central idea in the epistle of James. "Who is wise and understanding among you? Let him show it by his good life, by deeds done in the humility that comes from wisdom. But if you harbor bitter envy and selfish ambition in your hearts, do not boast about it or deny the truth. Such 'wisdom' does not come down from heaven but is earthly, unspiritual, of the devil. For where you have envy and selfish ambition, there you find disorder and every evil practice. But the wisdom that comes from heaven is first of all pure; then peace-loving, considerate, submissive, full of mercy and good fruit, impartial and sincere. Peacemakers who sow in peace raise a harvest of righteousness" (James 3:13-18).

Notice that this passage begins with a question: "Who is wise and understanding among you?" The Greek word translated "wise" in this verse (*sophos*) refers not to academic knowledge but to someone who has moral insight and skill in handling the affairs of his daily life. One's possession of real wisdom is shown by a godly life filled with good deeds and not by mere claim, argument, or display of university diplomas.

A man who has spent his entire life in mastering many provinces of learning, or who is familiar with some of the great realms of science, may have no wisdom, and a peasant who can barely read may be a wise man. The wise man has discovered the actual truth about the world and the order of human life. He has seen, and he never forgets,

God's invisible and eternal kingdom by which he is environed. He knows that for him and for all men the will of God is supreme. He has, therefore, the power and habit of forming a just judgment on wealth and poverty, joy and sorrow, ease and pain, public honor and public dishonor, and all the incidents of human experience. He has a clear vision of the laws that should regulate conduct, and of the principles that form character (*The Speaker's Bible*, "James," p. 141).

As James points out, Christians who glory in the attainment of worldly wisdom begin to create problems for themselves and for the entire church. Now this is not to say that it is wrong for a Christian to seek an education or to achieve excellence in his profession. Rather, it is wrong to parade these attainments and to depreciate brethren who have not had these opportunities. This type of behavior creates "jealousy" and "faction." There is no wisdom in such conduct.

A similar situation sometimes occurs in families. A son or daughter may surpass the parents of that home in terms of years of formal education. Add to this the praise that such a young person receives and the pride he may begin to take in himself and problems may surface in the family. He may become resentful of his parents' authority over him and begin to rebel. At the least, he may assume the role of a "smart aleck" and behave disrespectfully toward them.

Elders and godly Christian parents have wisdom which has been developed over years of spiritual experience in the service of Christ. They have seen and come to understand things that younger church members or children in the home have not had time to learn. This is why God gave them decision-making authority instead of turning over the leadership of these two divine institutions to younger people. This is God's arrangement and must be respected.

The pseudo-wisdom of the world which produces arrogance and strife among its claimants is, according to James, "earthly, unspiritual, of the devil."

71

The Nature of True Wisdom

The contrast between the pseudo-wisdom of the world and true wisdom "from above" (cf. James 1:17) is striking. James expands on the nature of true wisdom in order to give his readers a graphic view of the choices open to them as free men.

Eight words are used to describe the wisdom which comes from God and which his people should seek. As you study these words, ask yourself whether each trait described is found in your life. Concentrate on ways whereby you can learn to display these characteristics in the future. You will be advancing toward wisdom as you do so. In fact, as you see the desirability of these eight traits you will most assuredly want to incorporate them into your life pattern.

First, true wisdom is *pure.* The Bible emphasizes the truth that the God we serve is wholly pure (1 John 3:3). It likewise teaches that those who would share his fellowship must participate in his purity. It will not fulfill our spiritual calling to purify the outside of the cup (i.e., give up certain especially glaring vices) and leave the inside dirty (i.e., hold onto our "secret" sins). This was the approach of the Pharisees to religion (cf. Matt. 23:25-26). We must seek the total purity of heart and life which can only come from a divine cleansing.

We are cleansed initially when we are baptized into Christ and washed by his blood (Acts 22:16; Rom. 6:3-4). But how do we keep clean? Is it inevitable that, as a woman cleaning house only for it to get dirty again, we shall get soiled by the world's spiritual pollution again? No, for the purity which comes through the blood of Christ is not a once-only thing which is received at baptism. It is a continuous purity. John writes that "the blood of Jesus, his Son, purifies (literally, keeps on purifying) us from all sin" (1 John 1:7). So long as a Christian has the wisdom to "walk in the light" and serve God with sincerity, Christ's blood

72

continually purifies him of any sin which may attempt to stain him.

Second, true wisdom is *peace-loving*. As surely as true wisdom brings about an individual's right relationship with God through purifying him by Christ's blood, so also does it exhibit itself in establishing right relationships with other human beings. Whereas worldly wisdom creates strife, divine wisdom produces peace. It causes one to have a loving heart and peaceable disposition that contributes to harmonious relationships. It will not allow him to "pick fights" or delight in needless controversy.

Third, true wisdom is *considerate*. The word in the original text (*epieikes*) is used in the Septuagint to describe God's own disposition. In his dealing with us, he has been kind and gentle rather than exacting the penalty we were due to pay because of our sin. This quality is needed in our relationships with one another.

> That is to say it is forbearing, patient under provocation, respectful of the feelings of others, considerate, moderate. It does not insist on its own rights, will listen to reason, and leans toward forgiveness. It is no stickler for the letter of the law. It seeks to avoid inflicting pain. It is fair and is always mindful of the feelings of others -- making the kind of allowances for others which it would like to have made for itself. (Foy Valentine, *Where the Action Is: Studies in James*, p. 111).

Fourth, true wisdom is *submissive*. This doesn't mean that a person is spineless or weak. It means instead that he is not so inflexible and unheeding that he cannot yield to someone else.

> It is approachable, conciliatory, and not stubborn. It can be persuaded. It is not rigid. It is not beyond appeal. It can hear. If such wisdom were abundant today, a multitude of serious personal, family, and social problems could be solved overnight. When children know their parents hear them, when minorities can be sure the majority sees them, when young people are persuaded that older people know they are there, and when the disinherited can find some

73

assurance that the establishment is not ignoring them, then initial relationships will have been established upon which yet stronger relationships can be built. (Valentine, *op. cit.*).

Fifth, true wisdom is *full of mercy*. It is compassionate to those who are in trouble. Whether they are suffering unjustly or through their own fault, the child of God imitates his Father's great example and feels pity and sympathy for them. And, still following heaven's example, he turns that mercy and compassion into action.

Sixth, true wisdom is *full of good fruit*. Compassion from a Christian goes beyond mere emotion to actual deeds of help. It is one thing to see a needy person, cluck your tongue, wag your head, and tell another how you felt sorry for that man. It is another thing to see a needy person and then sacrifice your time, money, and energy to help him. How did the Good Samaritan "show mercy" to the wounded man lying beside the road? (cf. Luke 10:37). How can we show mercy to the people of our acquaintance who are in difficulty?

One Sunday morning I was driving to the church building to preach and passed by a poor family of my acquaintance whose car had broken down. I was in such a hurry to get to the building in order to sing and preach about my religion that I drove right by them. Before going far, I realized that I was practicing a shoddy religion if it would let me do that. I turned around. The wisdom from above will not allow us to substitute good wishes for good deeds.

Seventh, true wisdom is *impartial*. Older translations use words such as "without variance" (ASV) as their translation here. A better way to render *adiakritos*, however, is with the word "impartiality" or "without favoritism." It calls attention to the fact that people who live by true wisdom avoid the sinful tendency to discriminate against others.

Eighth, true wisdom is *sincere*. It is honest. It does not pretend to be what it is not. It does not put on disguises in order to conceal aims or motives that are unworthy.

74

The Need for Such Wisdom

Does our world need the true wisdom that is from above? Who can deny it?

Not everyone can have the IQ of a genius. Very few will have the opportunity to achieve notoriety in science, education, or the professional world. But everyone can have the wisdom described by James in this very beautiful passage. We can all submit ourselves humbly to God and live under his control. We can have the purity of heart and life which are necessary unto salvation and demonstrate the traits of character which flow from salvation. These are all gifts from God which are ours for the receiving.

Conclusion

There is a key issue which must not be overlooked as we contemplate how we may share in the true wisdom discussed in this chapter. Why do some go the path of selfish and arrogant "wisdom of the world"? Why do others -- relatively few by comparison -- follow the "wisdom from above"? The Scripture says: "The fear of the Lord is the beginning of wisdom; all who follow his precepts have good understanding" (Psa. 111:10). *Read*

Those who fear God and keep his commandments have true wisdom. They are able to live constructively and happily. They know the real meaning of life and see things in their proper perspective. But those who are without such reverent humility in the presence of the Almighty regard his commandments as foolishness and insist on going their own way unto destruction.

What is Christian living all about? It is emptying ourselves of pride and nurturing a spirit of humble reverence and obedience to God. It is learning that the path of reliance on God rather than on ourselves is true wisdom. It is "wising up" to the fact that we cannot chart our own

75

course in life and do as we please but that life's meaning is found in following the path marked by our Savior.

Memorize: Job 28:28

TAKE THOUGHT
1. Distinguish between knowledge and wisdom. Is this distinction obvious in the lives of people?
2. How does false wisdom of the world affect people? What situation does it create for its possessor and the people around him? Cf. 1 Cor. 3:19-20; Isa. 29:14.
3. Discuss the eight characteristics of true wisdom given by James. Are you developing these traits in your life?
4. Read Isaiah 11:2-5. Of whom does this passage speak? Should his wisdom not be found in his followers?
5. What is the "key" to attaining true wisdom? *Ask God*
James 1 V5

TAKE ACTION
1. Has education solved our problems in America? Why can it never do so by itself? Why has our own effort at being well-educated not solved our fundamental problems?
2. Write down your goals for life. Look at them carefully in light of this lesson and be sure you are planning with wisdom.

I Cor 3 v 19-20
2. foolishness w/ God

Isa

4. Speaks of Jesus

Chapter 8

The Cure for Conflict
James 4:1-10

Humanity is caught up in a near-constant state of unrest, quarreling, hatred, jealousy, and war.

Whole nations periodically go to war with each other. When there is peace among the nations, there remains the internal strife between black and white or labor and management among our nation's own people. When there is peace within a nation, there is strife between husband and wife or parent and child within our homes. When there is peace within the family unit, there occasionally surfaces a struggle among brethren which turns the church into a battleground.

Many people despair of ever finding real peace and simply assume that conflict is an inevitable part of life. Is this fatalistic view the correct one? Must we view life this way and resign ourselves to living it as warfare?

The Bible says that our warring world is the logical consequence of the countless wars that rage within men's hearts. Man fights with his fellow man because he cannot be at peace within his own heart. The lusts and evil deeds which alienate us from God also alienate ourselves from the people around us and set us to fighting. Thus it is that if we would have peace with one another we must first be at peace within our own beings -- at peace with God through Jesus Christ.

The Source of Conflict

James declares that the root cause of all our strife and conflict is *evil desire*. "What causes fights and quarrels among you: Don't they come from your desires that battle within you?" (James 4:1).

77

Our Lord taught this same truth in the Parable of the Soils. The cares and pleasures of this life, he said, serve to choke the gospel. They smother the Word of God, cause one to neglect spiritual things in favor of worldly things, and turn him back to sin. "The seed that fell among thorns stands for those who hear, but as they go on their way they are choked by life's worries, riches and pleasures, and they do not mature" (Luke 8:14).

When one becomes a slave to his lusts (i.e., evil desires), envy and hatred enter his life. Conflict with others is inevitable. "At one time we too were foolish, disobedient, deceived and enslaved by all kinds of passions and pleasures. We lived in malice and envy, being hated and hating one another" (Tit 3:3). Others seeking the same worldly goal or carnal pleasure become competitors to be beaten. This causes one to do all sorts of shameful and wicked things to others. "You want something but don't get it. You kill and covet, but you cannot have what you want. You quarrel and fight. You do not have, because you do not ask God" (James 4:2).

For a Christian man, his goal may be success and money in his business or profession. If he turns from righteousness and develops an evil desire for success at any price, he may sacrifice his principles and produce a cheap and inferior product to sell at an inflated price. Or he may resort to shady and unethical business practices in marketing his product or beating out his competitor. He may lie, cheat, or commit any number of other sinful acts.

For a Christian boy, his goal may be a certain class office or acceptance by a particular group of his peers. In order to attain his goal, he may have to close his eyes to certain things that he knows to be wrong or even compromise himself by some degree of participation in them. He may use bad language or tell dirty jokes to prove he is no "sissy" or "religious freak."

For a Christian woman, her goal may be career achievements at the sacrifice of her commitment to her family. It may be social standing within the community. It may be a lifestyle that is beyond the resources she and her husband have. In any one of these settings, she may set aside values she knows to be right in order to manipulate people and circumstances to her end.

For a Christian girl, her goal may be popularity and frequent dates. Depending on the group with which she seeks her popularity, she may lower her standards to dress immodestly or experiment with alcohol and other drugs or behave promiscuously in order to be accepted.

In all these cases, and with countless other similar examples which could be given, an evil desire (i.e., either a desire for something sinful in itself or the satisfaction of some legitimate desire by a sinful method) caused one to begin a downward spiral of wickedness. Each step down this path causes one to experience more guilt and to feel more keenly his separation from God and men. Each step involves him in more turmoil.

A Christian who gives way to evil desire has broken his vow to God. "You adulterous people, don't you know that friendship with the world is hatred toward God: Anyone who chooses to be a friend of the world becomes an enemy of God" (James 4:4). The church is Christ's bride (2 Cor. 11:2), and every member of the church is pledged to be faithful to Jesus as Lord. Thus it is that when Christians exhibit desire for and make compromises with the world they are guilty of *spiritual adultery*. They have taken love, energy, and time that belonged to Christ and have squandered it on the world. They have broken a covenant commitment.

The Cure for Conflict

What is the solution to this critical problem? How can one be at peace with God, himself, and people around him?

How can he maintain unquestioned loyalty to Christ in order to fulfill his covenant vow of faithfulness to God?

James answers by saying that one must submit himself totally to God and his will and consciously resist the devil and his snares. "Or do you think Scripture says without reason that the spirit he caused to live in us envies intensely? But he gives us more grace. That is why Scripture says: 'God opposes the proud but gives grace to the humble.' Submit yourselves, then, to God. Resist the devil, and he will flee from you" (James 4:5-7).

First, the Christian struggles against and, by the grace of God, overcomes his evil desires. One of the great destroyers of peace of mind is the desire for things to which a Christian knows he has no legitimate right. Whether the lust is for material things (1 Tim. 6:19-20) or for sensual pleasure (1 John 2:15-17), the child of God recognizes that the craving is antagonistic to spirituality. He knows that these desires "war against your soul" (cf. 1 Pet. 2:11), so he tries to be content with the opportunities and blessings God provides him and "keeps the lid on" his selfish impulses. By the power of God's indwelling Spirit, he resists the devil.

Second, he prays. One who is serving self cannot pray. He short-circuits the route of prayer by his sin. But the Christian who is striving against his evil desires and sincerely trying to do right can pray for God's strength and aid in the assurance of receiving an answer.

Third, he believes the Scripture and heeds its warnings and exhortations. Whereas the person who is serving self rather than God may act as if "Scripture says without reason" that evil desires destroy us, the faithful Christian knows that to reject the Word of God is to reject the Lord himself (cf. John 12:48). Rather than being proud and puffed up against the truth, the right-thinking child of God humbles himself and submits to divine counsel in all things.

If our rejection of [God's] claim for our full devotion is high-handed, arrogant and careless, as though we have a perfect right to run our lives just as we wish, then we shall be made to learn the painful truth declared in Scripture (in Prov. 3:34) that GOD OPPOSES THE PROUD. If, however, our failure to give God His due springs not from arrogant defiance and stubborn unconcern for His claims, but from our human frailty and weakness, so that we come before Him penitent and ashamed, we shall find that 'there is forgiveness with Him': HE GIVES GRACE TO THE HUMBLE, that is, forgiveness for the past and delivering power for the future. (C. Leslie Mitton, *The Epistle of James*, p. 157).

Yes, one's salvation and experience of peace is attributable to God's infinite grace. We achieve neither because of what we are but receive both because of the mercy of the Almighty. But he bestows such mercy only on the striving, prayerful, believing child of God who comes humbly to receive a free gift. He forces it on no one.

The Disposition Which Makes for Peace

It is not that we shall ever achieve perfection in this life. Neither is it that we take sin lightly and regard our failures as matters of no consequence. Rather it is a matter of one's heart and disposition before God. This is why James closes this section of text with a description of the disposition which makes for peace. "Come near to God and he will come near to you. Wash your hands, you sinners, and purify your hearts, you double-minded. Grieve, mourn and wail. Change your laughter to mourning and your joy to gloom. Humble yourselves before the Lord, and he will lift you up" (James 4:8-10).

In Christ there is a priesthood of all believers (cf. 1 Pet. 2:9). Every Christian has constant access to God through Christ. But, as was typified by the purity required of the Old Testament priests, only the Christian who is pure before God can legitimately exercise his office. Only the Christian possessed of such purity can have the peace which God gives his faithful people.

The command is "Come near to God . . ." The prerequisites of doing so are (1) a pure life, (2) a pure heart, (3) a penitent spirit, and (4) humility.

First, to "wash your hands" is to cease all conscious acts of wrongdoing. It is to purify one's whole life of any evil still being tolerated in it.

Second, to "purify your hearts" is to cleanse the inner spring of life. For one to contend that it does not matter what goes on in his heart so long as his actions are respectable is to be guilty of doublemindedness (cf. Matt. 7:21-23).

Third, to "grieve, mourn and wail" is to be truly penitent and sober as one comes before God. While James does not deny the joy of the Christian life, he stresses that one cannot be casual or frivolous about his religion. "Here the laughter which is rebuked is . . . the flippant laughter of careless unconcern in the presence of facts which more properly should induce grief and remorse" (Mitton, *op. cit.*, p. 162).

Fourth, to "humble yourselves before the Lord" is to realize that we are the creatures and God is the Creator. This gives us a frame of mind conducive to obedience. It causes us to understand our role as servants who are to carry out not our own wills but the will of our Father in heaven. The humble person will be exalted by his God (cf. Matt. 23:12).

For one to have such a disposition as this is so very rare. Yet it is within the power of every child of God to develop and manifest these traits. Purity of actions and motives is possible through the blood of Christ. Mourning over our own sins and those of the world comes as a direct result of such cleansing, for one who no longer desires or participates in sin can see its hideousness with objectivity and as God himself views it. Humility then comes as we attempt to serve God daily in a world filled with sin and obstacles to spirituality. And what is the fruit of such a disposition? *Peace.*

Conclusion

What conflicts are causing you problems? Maybe you are having trouble getting along with people where you work. Or maybe your conflicts are with the members of your own family. Do you have trouble maintaining friendships? Does the whole world seem to be down on you?

Before blaming everyone else for your troubles and inability to get along, look at yourself. Is your disposition one that makes for peace? Or are you a "hothead" who loses his temper too easily? Do you always have to be right? Can you admit your mistakes and apologize to people whom you offend?

What is Christian living all about? It is the conquering of evil desires which lead one into all sorts of hatred, malice, and conflict. It is the purging out of one's heart all the cares and pleasures of the world which destroy spirituality. It is the creation of a holy and peaceable disposition, character- ized by humility, penitence, and purity of heart and life. It is the cultivation of a disposition which gives one peace -- with his God, with his fellow men, and with his own spirit.

Memorize: James 4:6-7

TAKE THOUGHT
1. What is the root of all strife and conflict? Can you illustrate this truth from your own experience?
2. Discuss James 4:4 in detail.   What is spiritual adultery? Familiarize yourself with the Old Testament book of Hosea. What is its message?
3. What are the three steps to conquering spiritual conflict and the evil desires which underlie it?
4. What four things are prerequisite to "coming near to God"? How does this disposition make for peace?
5. Discuss Galatians 5:24 in detail.

TAKE ACTION
1. Secure a copy of *None of These Diseases* by S. I. McMillen. Read chapter 10 and discuss it in class.

2. Who are the people with whom you have the most difficulty getting along? Have you shown the disposition which makes for peace toward them? Will you take some positive steps to make peace with them?

3. How do the matters discussed in this chapter relate to mental health? How much mental illness could be cured if people would heed the Word of God? Help someone struggling with conflict to learn this important lesson.

Chapter 9

Don't Leave God Out of Your Plans
James 4:13-17

Before reading even one more line of this chapter, answer this question: What are your dreams, plans, and goals for the future?

What type of answer did you give? Completing your education? Getting married? Beginning a family? Traveling to distant places? A new car? Becoming president of your company? Getting rich? Being elected to public office? Becoming famous?

Or do you interpret life in terms of spiritual considerations -- salvation, spiritual growth, service rendered, heaven and hell?

Too many people place the emphasis in all the wrong places when they think about the future and what they will do with their lives. We are prone to be too earth-bound in our thinking and to leave God out of our plans. Jesus taught: "But seek first his kingdom and his righteousness, and all these things will be given you as well" (Matt. 6:33).

The Holy Spirit led James to rebuke the arrogance and self-sufficiency which characterize mankind. "Now listen, you who say, 'Today or tomorrow we will go to this or that city, spend a year there, carry on business and make money.' Why you do not even know what will happen tomorrow. What is your life? You are a mist that appears for a little while and then vanishes. Instead, you ought to say, 'If it is the Lord's will, we will live and do this or that.' As it is, you boast and brag. All such boasting is evil. Anyone, then, who knows the good he ought to do and doesn't do it, sins." (James 4:13-17).

We must not exclude God from our thinking. We must learn to give primary emphasis to his will for our lives and to his divine providence.

Heaven Is Involved in Our Affairs

The Bible both presupposes and clearly teaches the fact of the providence of God. The psalmist assumes the providence of God in such statements as are found in Psalm 3:5 and 55:22. "I lie down and sleep; I wake again, because the Lord sustains me." "Cast your cares on the Lord and he will sustain you; he will never let the righteous fall." The writer of these two verses did not explain his life in terms of mere naturalistic processes or chance occurrences. Even so normal an event as sleeping and waking was associated with the power of God. Therefore he could easily believe that the Lord would sustain and protect him in every other affair of life on Earth.

In an even clearer statement of the Lord's ability and willingness to exercise his providential care over the lives of his people, Jesus said, "Therefore I tell you, do not worry about your life, what you will eat; or about your body, what you will wear. Life is more than food, and the body more than clothes. Consider the ravens: They do not sow or reap, they have no storeroom or barn; yet God feeds them. And how much more valuable you are than birds! Who of you by worrying can add a single hour to his life? Since you cannot do this very little thing, why do you worry about the rest? . . . And do not set your heart on what you will eat or drink; do not worry about it. For the pagan world runs after all such things, and your Father knows that you need them. But seek his kingdom, and these things will be given to you as well" (Luke 12:22-31).

Then there is the familiar statement from Paul regarding the providence of God: "And we know that in all things God works for the good of those who love him, who have been called according to his purpose" (Rom. 8:28).

These are only a few of many Scriptures which assert the providential care of God over his people. This fact of God's promised care, when properly understood, is one of the most precious of all the promises that God has ever made to his children. The person who correctly understands and applies the truths contained in Scripture concerning the providence of God is able to have a great deal more confidence about his daily living than the person who lacks that understanding. He is able to face each day of his life with the confident assurance that God is aware of his every action and need, that God cares for his welfare, and that God will -- consistent with his purpose to save him -- provide all the things he needs to live acceptably in his service.

Difficulty of Believing in God's Providence

Those of us who counsel others as they face difficult situations in life realize that many people find it practically impossible to believe that God personally oversees their lives for good. Without this firm confidence in God's power and willingness to see after the welfare of his children, such people are depressed and despondent over their prospects. They cannot see their way out of troubles, and they have failed to rely on God for his strength and help. Perhaps our emphasis that miracles were confined to the first and second generations of the church's existence has left the impression with some that God is not doing anything in the world of our own time. But providence, as will be shown later in this study, is not miraculous in its nature. Therefore it was not confined to the earliest days of the church. Providence is a non-miraculous, indirect intervention of God which is sufficient to accomplish his divine purposes in human affairs.

There are other reasons of a more practical nature why people find it difficult to believe in God's overruling power in the lives of Christian people. There is the desolation which we often find in nature. In certain years farmers spend thousands of dollars preparing soil, planting crops, fertilizing fields, and protecting them against insects with expensive insecticides only to watch a terrible drought

87

destroy everything they have done. Or, if not a drought, perhaps a flash flood sweeps everything away in a matter of a few hours. When people are forced to see or experience such tragedies as these, they often find it very difficult to believe that God is overruling all things for good.

Then there are such things as famine and war in our world. It is estimated that 50 percent of the world's population goes to bed hungry every night. It is heartbreaking to see pictures on television or in newspapers of tiny children who are scarcely more than skeletons. Their parents are either too poor to give them the food they need or else they don't know enough about nutrition to provide the kinds of food they need.

There is the awful tragedy of war. Homes are destroyed, whole families are uprooted with nowhere to go, young soldiers are cut down on battlefields in the Middle East, in Northern Ireland, in Central America.

In view of all these tragic things that are constantly happening in our world, can intelligent people still believe in an all-powerful and loving God who is in control of all things? Can we believe that he overrules all things for the good of his people?

Definition of Providence

The *New Century Dictionary* defines providence as "the foreseeing care and guardianship of God over his creatures." I believe this definition is accurate up to a point, but we must clarify one matter.

God's control and supervision over human affairs in order to bring the highest good to men is not promised to all men. It is promised only to Christians -- "for the good of those who love him, who have been called according to his purpose" (Rom. 8:28). Thus providence may be defined as *God's control and supervision of all the events of our world to bring the highest good to his saved people.*

Now this is not to say that God causes all things to happen. He does not. Many men do things that are contrary to the will of God. Sometimes even Christians do things that are in violation of the Lord's revealed will for them. God does not cause all things to happen, for each of his human creatures has a free will and is free to choose the good or the evil, to choose to obey the laws of God or to disobey them. But the biblical doctrine of providence presupposes the ability of God to take whatever does happen and use that event to the ultimate accomplishment of his holy purposes.

The Age of Second Causes

We live in what someone has called "The Age of Reliance on Second Causes." That is simply another way of saying that men generally have a purely naturalistic concept of life which does not take God's workings into account.

If you were to ask the "man on the street" about the cause of successful living, what do you think you would hear? One would say that money is the key to success. "If a man has enough money, he can do anything, be anything, get anything he wants." Another person might respond to your inquiry by saying that education is the secret. "Give a kid four years of college and put him through a professional school, and he's got it made." Still others would assign success to such things as political philosophy, housing, food, or health. None of these things, nor all of them taken together, can legitimately be made the cause of the ultimate outcome of a man's life. These are mere secondary considerations.

To clarify the difference between primary and secondary causes, perhaps the following illustration will be helpful. When you walk into your house and flick the light switch, what illuminates the house? Does your finger on a switch really have that much power? Of course not. That is only a secondary cause. What ultimately causes your house to be illuminated is a powerful dynamo which is miles and miles away from your home.

So it is with human life. Education, money, housing, and health all can contribute a part in bringing happiness and success to people. But they are all secondary factors. The real cause of a man's success in life is God, the One who generates all that is good. "Every good and perfect gift is from above, coming down from the Father of the heavenly lights" (James 1:17).

Humanity must be restored to faith in the ultimate First Cause, God. Rather than attribute their good fortune to luck or fate, let men instead praise God from whom all blessings flow. When things are going badly, again let men assign rightful causes. We live in a world where sin abounds to thwart God's purposes in isolated instances. But let the Christian continue to trust God to ultimately "work all things together for good" in his life.

James addressed himself to this problem of how to view the affairs of everyday life by describing some hypothetical businessmen who are discussing their plans. "Now listen, you who say, 'Today or tomorrow we will go to this or that city, spend a year there, carry on business and make money.' Why, you do not even know what will happen tomorrow. What is your life? You are a mist that appears for a little while and then vanishes away. Instead, you ought to say, 'If it is the Lord's will, we will live and do this or that' " (James 4:13-15). The rebuke of this passage is not directed toward wise planning or to the nature of the business in which the men were engaged or to the fact that they anticipated a profit. The rebuke was aimed at the fact that God had been ignored in their planning.

One man attributes everything to naturalistic processes. He views his business in terms of his skill as a trader, his good timing in evaluating the market, etc. The other attributes everything to God and says, "If the Lord will, I shall do this or that and such will be the outcome." The former views himself as the first cause in everything; the latter acknowledges that all things are subject to the will and power of God. Where is your faith? In secondary causes or in the ultimate First Cause?

"If the Lord Will . . ."

James continued and said, in effect, "Before boasting of tomorrow, think about the nature of earthly life. Is life on the morrow assured? Is life permanent?" He answered his question by saying, "You are a mist." Life is like steam, a mist, or a puff of smoke. It is here only briefly and then is gone. With life so uncertain as this, how foolish we are to plan the future without regard to him who holds the future in his hands.

"Instead, you ought to say, 'If it is the Lord's will . . .'" It is not that we are required to use these words as a formula in our speech. James is rather enjoining an attitude of heart -- whether expressed or implied -- that gives God his rightful place in the planning and ordering of our lives. To plan is right and good. Only let the knowledge that God's will must prevail be firmly fixed in our minds. When it becomes apparent that our wills are in conflict with the Lord's, let us humbly submit to his providential guidance (cf. Prov. 3:6; Acts 18:21; 1 Cor. 4:19).

In all your ways acknowledge Him

James closes this section with an appeal and warning. "As it is, you boast and brag. All such boasting is evil. Anyone, then, who knows the good he ought to do and doesn't do it, sins" (James 4:16-17). Those who refuse to renounce their arrogance and to submit humbly to God's will are refusing to do good. They commit sin by having such an arrogant spirit, and they thwart God's intention to bless them.

Conclusion

Your life is a gift from God and is to be used for his glory. "Now all has been heard; here is the conclusion of the matter: Fear God, and keep his commandments; for this is the whole duty of man" (Eccl. 12:13). Thus it is that you cannot afford to make the mistake of trying to plan your future without God's help.

What is Christian living all about? It is a humble realization that one's life is not his own. It is a recognition that he has been "bought at a price" and has as his goal in life to "honor God" in all things (1 Cor. 6:19-20). It is an appreciation of the fact that all things are under the ultimate control of Almighty God and that his life has meaning only in relation to the divine will.

Memorize: Matthew 6:33 *But seek first the kingdom of God and all these things will be added to you.*

TAKE THOUGHT

1. Have you learned to interpret life in terms of spiritual considerations? What differences has this made in your life?

2. What is *providence*? Show that the Bible teaches that God is involved in human events.

3. Do you think "The Age of Reliance on Second Causes" is a correct designation of our time? How does this spirit show itself?

4. Discuss the significance of the phrase "If the Lord will."

5. What is your primary goal in life? Do all your other plans fit with this purpose? By what method do you intend to achieve your goal?

TAKE ACTION

1. Talk to some of your non-Christian friends about their plans and goals for life. Lead them into a discussion of James 4:13-17 and its application to their spiritual needs.

2. Pray fervently and regularly for God's will to be done in your life. Don't fight God by refusing to do what you know is right.

Chapter 10

Does Money Buy Everything?
James 5:1-6

The rich are very often the objects of other people's envy. The man who drives a Mercedes, wears custom-tailored clothes, flashes expensive jewelry, and owns half the town will likely turn everybody's head. People will look at him and wish they could swap places with him. They will fantasize about what it would be like to have his lifestyle. This unqualified yearning for money and the things it can buy is *spiritually unhealthy*.

In the Bible, the rich are often the objects of divine scorn and condemnation. "But woe to you that are rich, for you have already received your comfort. Woe to you who are well fed now, for you will go hungry. Woe to you who laugh now, for you will mourn and weep" (Luke 6:24-25). "And Jesus looked at him and said, How hard it is for the rich to enter the kingdom of God!" (Luke 18:24).

The point of such stinging rebukes is not to teach that there is sin in being rich or merit in being poor. It is God who gives certain of his people the power to achieve wealth (cf. Deut. 8:18), and abundant increase is sometimes the sign of his special favor upon an individual (e.g., Abraham). The Word of God also recognizes that poverty is sometimes caused by laziness and forbids the church to relieve a person in such circumstances (cf. 2 Thess. 3:10). What, then, is the Bible's teaching about earthly riches?

It is simply that *we are not to put our primary trust in riches but in the God who gives all things.* "Whoever trusts in his riches will fall, but the righteous will thrive like a green leaf" (Prov. 11:28). This was the gist of Jesus' teaching when he said, "Do not store up for yourselves treasures on earth, where moth and rust destroy, and where thieves break in and steal. But store up for yourselves treasures in heaven, where moth and rust do not destroy, and where thieves do not break in and steal. For where your treasure is, there your heart will be also" (Matt. 6:19-21).

> It is more than apparent that James does not criticize the rich simply because they are rich. There is here the presupposition . . . that they had made their money deceitfully and spent it only on themselves. Riches can be a blessing or they can be a terrible curse. It all depends on how they are acquired and how they are spent. As someone has said, there are four classes of people when it comes to the matter of possessions: (1) those who are rich in this world's goods and poor toward God; (2) those who are poor in this world and rich toward God; (3) those who are poor both in this world and the next; (4) those who have a considerable amount of this world's goods, but because they hold them with a loose hand are rich in the next world, also. But this class is not very numerous. (Spiros Zodhiates, *The Behavior of Belief*, III, 37).

In James 5:1-6, the Holy Spirit seeks to impress two important truths. First, this text shows the ultimate worthlessness of earthly riches. Contrary to popular opinion, money does not buy everything. Second, it shows the depravity of soul which results when one does put his trust in worldly goods rather than in God. In the materialistic world we inhabit, hardly any warnings could be more timely.

Miseries of Materialism

"Now listen, you rich people, weep and wail because of the misery that is coming upon you" (James 5:1). The rich people addressed in this passage are not Christians. James does not call them "brethren" but simply as "you rich." But was this epistle not written to Christians? Why address such a stern rebuke to non-Christian rich people in a letter sent to those who were Christians? For the precise reason indicated in the opening paragraph of this chapter. They are denounced severely so that Christians will be warned against envying them.

The rich may seem comfortable and secure. Their lifestyle may include all the luxuries that anyone could possibly imagine. But if the non-Christian rich people knew what "misery" was ahead of them they would "weep and wail." Whatever other calamities may have been implied in James' original statement here, it is certain that the destruction of these people in the day of final Judgment was included. For, in spite of the fact that money will buy many things, it will not buy one's spiritual security when he stands before the Judge of Heaven and Earth.

"Your wealth has rotted, and moths have eaten your clothes. Your gold and your silver are corroded. Their corrosion will testify against you and eat your flesh like fire. You have hoarded wealth in the last days" (James 5:2-3). In ancient times, riches fell into three main categories, i.e., foodstuffs, expensive apparel, and precious metals. Thus James emphasized the impermanence of each category in turn. The highly perishable "riches" of food and grain would rot. Expensive "clothes" would be eaten by moths. Their precious "gold" and "silver," though these metals do not actually rust, would deteriorate in beauty and value until they were consumed. "Their corrosion," wrote James, "will testify against you" that you have placed your trust in the wrong things.

The loss of these things would, he added, "eat your flesh as fire." That is, it would bring complete ruin upon the people who had put their confidence in them, for they had nothing else on which to rely.

Then comes the somewhat difficult statement: "You have hoarded wealth in the last days." Men have been living in "the last days" since that Pentecost Day on which the church was established. James may be saying that the hoarding of wealth in this era, as opposed to putting it to use for God's purposes, is sinful. Or he may be using irony to suggest that such materialists were, by their unspiritual use of money and goods, laying up a "treasure" of wrath for

95

themselves (cf. Rom. 2:5). In either case, nothing complimentary is intended or implied.

Some Sins Related to Materialism

Some terrible sins are frequently associated with materialism. "People who want to get rich fall into temptation and a trap and into many foolish and harmful desires that plunge men into ruin and destruction. For the love of money is a root of all kinds of evil . . ." (1 Tim. 6:9-10a).

James identifies and comments on three of these sins in verses 4-6. "Look! The wages you failed to pay workmen who mowed your fields are crying against you. The cries of the harvesters have reached the ears of the Lord Almighty. You have lived on earth in luxury and self-indulgence. You have fattened yourselves in the day of slaughter. You have condemned and murdered innocent men, who were not opposing you."

First, he refers to *injustice.* One who agrees to pay another to do a particular job for him is under condemnation if he does not pay fairly. Under the Law of Moses, an employer was not allowed to hold a poor man's wages past sundown (Deut. 24:14-15). The prophets Jeremiah and Malachi pronounced divine judgment against those who oppressed hired servants or refused to pay wages justly earned (Jer. 22:13; Mal. 3:5). Jesus reminded us that the "worker deserves his wages" (Luke 10:7).

The person who loves money and who is concerned only about the profit he can clear for himself does not hesitate to ignore these warnings against injustice to his employees. Thus it is that some people are forced to work under unsafe conditions, to accept shamefully low wages, and to suffer other wrongs at the hands of unscrupulous men. Labor movements and federal laws have done away with many -- but by no means all -- the injustices tied to economic exploitation. Such things will be totally eliminated only when the hearts of men are changed by the power of God.

> There seems always to have been an employer and an employee. There must have been an original capitalist who put his capital to work for him, and in order to do that he had to hire servants or laborers. The existence of these two groups of people does not seem to be condemned by the Word of God. What is condemned, however, is the exploitation of the worker by the employer and vice versa. Because the primary target here is the employer, it does not mean that he is necessarily the only one at fault in the dispute which exists in our management-labor relationships. The loafing worker is condemned just as much. There is an established principle of justice and respect for the rights of each other. The employer should not forget that the employee is entitled to a decent wage, and the employee should recognize the right of the employer to make a reasonable profit. If each one recognized and defended the rights of the other as much as his own, what a wonderful relationship there would be between these two groups whose cooperation is so essential to the production of that which is necessary for the sustenance of life. (Zodhiates, *op. cit.*, p. 64).

Second, he speaks of *selfishness*. Verse five pictures materialistic people and their desire for luxury and "self-indulgence" (i.e., lewdness and impurity). They flagrantly forget and ignore the needs of others in order to gratify their lusts. They trample others' rights in order to live what they consider "the good life."

The mass media combine to create the impression in the minds of most people of this generation that to work less and play more is the ideal state of life for which we should strive. All of us are being urged to think and behave selfishly. To the degree that one of us falls into this trap of abandoning productive labor for selfish leisure, he or she loses the ability to live for any other reason. Worldly luxury and pleasure are not the goals for which we should aim. Focusing on and becoming involved in this world's pleasures distracts from the pursuit of spiritual things.

Why is it that fewer people attend Sunday evening services and Wednesday night Bible study than attend Sunday morning "preaching service"? Why is it so hard to recruit people to teach Sunday School classes? Why do so few visit the sick or attempt to evangelize the lost? These things cut into our leisure activities and force us to choose between living spiritually or selfishly. And our generation is so generally materialistic that it will, as a rule, choose the selfish over the spiritual. "The worries of this life, the deceitfulness of wealth and desires for other things come in and choke the word, making it unfruitful." (Mark 4:19).

Third, James points out that *murder* is frequently associated with materialism. Those who would unjustly deny one his wages in order to live in selfish pleasure could easily become involved in actual murder in order to steal another's money or property. The wicked and selfish Ahab murdered Naboth in order to get possession of the latter's fine vineyard (1 Kings 21). The same thing (i.e., murder with robbery as the motive) happens every day in our country. The notorious drug trafficking which makes daily headlines is nothing less than evil people willing to kill others for the sake of money.

It can also be observed that to cheat a poor man and take away his living (cf. v. 4) is to murder him. It is to take away the things that are necessary for him and his family to live. It may even be that James was saying every such injustice heaped upon Christ's people is another wound to Christ (i.e., the Righteous One) himself.

The Rich Young Ruler

One of the most familiar episodes in the life of Jesus involves his encounter with a rich young ruler. The young man ran to Jesus and asked about the prerequisites of eternal life. The Savior told the young man -- who was a Jew living under the Law of Moses -- that he would have to keep the Ten Commandments. The eager young man replied, "All these I have kept since I was a boy."

Then Jesus, looking into the man's heart, saw that the one thing which would serve to keep him out of heaven was covetousness. That young man, like so many young men of this generation, was too wrapped up in the pursuit of money and possessions. Therefore Jesus said, "You still lack one thing. Sell everything you have and give it to the poor, and you will have treasure in heaven. Then come, follow me."

Before he could be saved, he would have to stop loving his money. Jesus told him to prove his once-for-all break with covetousness by selling everything he owned and giving it to the poor. Does that sound too difficult to you? It affirms the absolute impossibility of someone being saved who is a covetous person.

What was the young ruler's reaction to the demand? "When he heard this, he became very sad, because he was a man of great wealth" (Luke 18:18-23). The rich young ruler left and, insofar as we are able to determine, never came back to Jesus. He forfeited his soul in order to keep his money.

When the rich young ruler's decision was apparent, Jesus turned to the disciples and said, "How hard it is for the rich to enter the kingdom of God! Indeed, it is easier for a camel to go through the eye of a needle than for a rich man to enter the kingdom of God" (Luke 18:24-25). There are some who have tried to explain away the significance of this statement by saying that the "eye of the needle" to which the Lord referred was a small gate in a wall. Thus they interpret him to be saying that just as a camel has to work diligently in order to get through such a small opening so a man like this rich young ruler would have to struggle in order to be saved. This is not what the Lord said. He said that it is utterly impossible for anyone with this young man's attitude toward material wealth to be saved.

Luke, in quoting the Lord, used a Greek word which denotes a sewing needle -- not a small gate. Luke was a physician and probably had in mind the type of needle which he would use to sew up a wound. Can a camel go through the eye of that type of needle? It would be impossible. So also is it impossible for one who loves money -- a covetous man -- to enter heaven.

Many religious people who are concerned over the present moral decline in this country and the world are speaking out against such things as drugs and illicit sex, but most seem to have accepted covetousness as an inherent part of American life. But this cannot be right in the sight of God. He is very severe with the sin of covetousness. Since this is God's attitude toward it, faithful children of God can have no other attitude toward covetousness. To fail to teach the truth on this subject will bring condemnation on those who presume to teach the will of God.

God's severity toward the sin of covetousness is seen in the fact that he struck both Ananias and Sapphira dead because of it (cf. Acts 5:1-10). Paul commanded the saints at Corinth to withdraw from and refuse even to eat with any brother in that church who was covetous (1 Cor. 5:11). Materialistic persons are forfeiting all hope of heaven in their feverish pursuit of this world.

Conclusion

Money cannot buy everything. It cannot buy health and happiness. It cannot buy a good name. It cannot buy trust and respect. It cannot buy love. It cannot buy God's favor or a home in heaven. These words from the pen of Paul are therefore good counsel: "Set your minds on the things above, not on earthly things. For you died, and your life is now hidden with Christ in God. When Christ, who is your life, appears, then you also will appear with him in glory" (Col. 3:2-4).

What is Christian living all about? It is seeing this world and the world to come in proper perspective. It is forfeiting selfish pleasures here in order to share eternal blessedness in the hereafter. It is viewing one's fellow men as souls of infinite worth before God and not as "rich" or "poor" to be catered to and taken advantage of accordingly. It is seeking the will of God above all other things and trusting him to provide adequately for our physical needs according to his promise.

Memorize: 1 Timothy 6:9

But those who desire to be rich fall into temptation & to a snare into many senseless & harmful desires that plunge people into ruin & destruction.

TAKE THOUGHT

1. Is it sinful to be rich? Is it sinful to be poor? Where does sin enter the picture with regard to money?

2. What two central truths are impressed on our minds by the text under consideration?

3. What are some of the sins commonly associated with materialism?

4. Discuss the story of the Rich Young Ruler. What good things can be said about him? What was Jesus' attitude toward him? Why did he fail to follow Jesus?

5. The following passages refer primarily to the use of money: 2 Cor. 9:6-15 and Gal. 6:7-10. Discuss them in detail. Do Christians generally give as if they believed these promises?

TAKE ACTION

1. Do some calculating on paper about the amount of money you have spent in the past month. How much was spent on clothes, cosmetics, movies, sports events, food, church contributions, etc.? If you saw these same figures about someone else's use of his money, would you consider him materialistic?

2. Read and investigate Malachi 3:8-9. In what way were these people robbing God? Can we rob God?

3. Are Christians under obligation to tithe? Of what law was tithing a part? What guidelines govern a Christian's giving? Should we give more or less than a tenth?

Chapter 11

Be Patient Until the Lord Comes
James 5:7-11

In the first verse of chapter five, a stinging rebuke had been directed to the non-Christian rich who had oppressed and humiliated the poor. At verse seven, James looks at the other side of the circumstance.

> James now turns from the 'rich' whose heartless conduct he has condemned, and addresses himself to his Christian 'brothers' who are the victims of such ill-treatment. His words are intended to bring them comfort and encouragement in the humiliations they are suffering and the exasperation and resentment which they cannot but feel. He pleads with them to BE PATIENT UNTIL THE COMING OF THE LORD" (C. Leslie Mitton, *The Epistle of James*, p. 183).

A Close Examination of the Text

First, there is a *command*. "Be patient, then, brothers, until the Lord's coming. See how the farmer waits for the land to yield its valuable crop and how patient he is for the autumn and spring rains. You too, be patient and stand firm, because the Lord's coming is near" (James 5:7-8). James has just assured his readers that the evil rich will be justly rewarded for their deeds. Now he assures the Christians who have suffered at their hands that they will be blessed. But they would have to be patient until the Lord actually comes to settle accounts.

As an illustration of the type of patience these early Christians needed, James called their attention to the farmer. A farmer does not reap his harvest the next day after planting. He knows the laws of nature concerning seed germination, plant growth, and fruit production. He expects to have to wait for this process to occur. In similar fashion, Christians who see injustices which need to be remedied must await the return of the Lord with a patient

103

spirit. As surely as the laws of seedtime and harvest are appointed of God, so also is the coming of Christ assured by the same God.

Second, there is an *appeal*. "Don't grumble against each other, brothers, or you will be judged. The judge is standing at the door" (James 5:9). In their state of oppression, these Christians were tempted to become fretful and impatient with one another. They were tempted to find fault with their brethren, blame them for their difficulties, and take quick offense with them. This type of attitude backfires upon one and must be avoided (cf. Matt. 7:1-5). Again, more patience and faith were needed.

Third, there is *encouragement* from historical examples of patience. "Brothers, as an example of patience in the face of suffering, take the prophets who spoke in the name of the Lord. As you know, we consider blessed those who have persevered. You have heard of Job's perseverance and have seen what the Lord finally brought about. The Lord is full of compassion and mercy" (James 5:10-11).

The prophets of God in Old Testament days often went unheeded as they declared the Word of God and frequently had to endure physical persecutions. To suffer for the sake of righteousness is not a hindrance to salvation but an aid. "Rejoice and be glad, because great is your reward in heaven, for in the same way they persecuted the prophets who were before you" (Matt. 5:12). Steadfastness under pressure is an evidence of the genuineness of one's faith and constitutes an assurance of his eternal salvation.

Job, though dreadfully tormented by various afflictions, forsaken by his friends, and crying out in agony over his calamities, "did not sin by charging God with wrongdoing" (Job 1:22). A faithful disciple of the Lord, following the example of Job, will endure any trial rather than forsake God.

Whether our situation today is one of joy or sorrow, we must patiently await the Lord's coming.

Jesus Is Coming Again

The New Testament has a great deal to say about the second coming of Christ. Just as the Old Testament is filled with the promise of his *first coming*, so the New Testament is filled with the promise of his *second coming*. So regularly did the writers of the New Testament speak of the second coming that one of every 25 verses in the entire book refers to it.

In the Old Testament period, the prophets spoke confidently of the coming of the Messiah. But as the years passed, the hope of the people grew dim. They came to doubt the promise of God. Then, when Christ finally did come, they were not expecting him, and they did not receive him. In similar fashion, the New Testament prophets spoke confidently of Christ's second coming. Nearly 2,000 years have come and gone since they first began making such prophecies, and the expectation of many people has perished.

Many people are now heard to question that promise, and not a few actually say that they do not believe it. It has happened, just as Peter predicted it would, that men scoff at the very idea of a literal second coming of Christ. "In the last days scoffers will come scoffing and following their own evil desires. They will say, 'Where is this coming he promised?' "(2 Pet. 3:3-4).

Just as surely as he came the first time, though, Christ is coming again. God's promises are not just so many vain words. They are the sure Word of an Almighty God. Every prophecy of the Scriptures must be fulfilled. "But do not forget this one thing, dear friends: With the Lord a day is like a thousand years, and a thousand years are like one day. The Lord is not slow in keeping his promise, as some understand slowness. He is patient with you not wanting anyone to perish, but everyone to come to repentance. But the day of the Lord will come like a thief. The heavens will disappear with a roar; the elements will be destroyed by fire, and the earth and everything in it will be laid bare. . . . So then, dear friends, since you are looking forward to this, make every effort to be found spotless, blameless and at peace with him" (2 Pet. 3:8-10, 14).

To Be Different from His First Coming

A study of some New Testament passages which speak of the second coming of Christ shows that it will be vastly different, in both manner and purpose, from his first coming.

Jesus' first coming was in humiliation. He had existed in heaven with the Father from eternity. In order to come among men, he "made himself nothing, taking the very nature of a servant, being made in human likeness. And being found in appearance as a man, he humbled himself, and became obedient to death -- even death on a cross" (Phil. 2:7-8). He was lied about, slandered, persecuted, and finally executed as a criminal. "In his humiliation he was deprived of justice. Who can speak of his descendants? For his life was taken from the earth" (Acts 8:33).

But as surely as his first coming was in humiliation, his second coming will be in glory. Every eye will see him (Rev. 1:7), every knee will bow before him, and every tongue will confess his name (Rom. 14:11). He will judge the world with justice (Acts 17:31). He emptied himself before coming to earth the first time, divested himself of his heavenly glory. When he returns, he will come in full splendor. "When the Son of man comes in his glory, and all the angels with him, he will sit on his throne in heavenly glory. All the nations will be gathered before him . . ." (Matt. 25:31-32).

The Time of His Second Coming

From the time of Christ's departure from Earth, men have been trying to determine the day and hour of his return. Paul spoke of men who sought to "beguile" and "trouble" the saints by teaching "that the day of the Lord has already come" (2 Thess. 2:2). There have been any number of men since that time who have drawn attention to themselves by their claims to have discovered the time of the Lord's return.

William Miller, a figure associated with the founding of Seventh-Day Adventism, set the date of Christ's second coming as sometime between March 21, 1843, and March 21, 1844. He based his prediction on a false interpretation of Daniel 8:14. He and a band of people who had believed his inaccurate teaching waited for the Lord's coming in vain. The year went by and nothing happened. They decided that they had made a mistake, so they recalculated the date and came up with October 22, 1844. Again they waited. Again nothing happened.

Charles T. Russell, founder of the Jehovah's Witness movement, said Christ would return in 1874 in an effort to popularize his movement. The Arab-Israeli War of 1967 set off a series of speculations about the second coming of Christ. Herbert W. Armstrong predicted Christ's return by 1975. A former NASA engineer named Edgar Whisenant caused a stir by writing *88 Reasons Why the Rapture Will Be In 1988* and predicted: "The Rapture will occur sometime during the period of Rosh-Hash-Ana, between sunset Sept. 11 and sunset, Sept. 13." All the predictors were wrong.

Listen to what Jesus said about all such attempts to set the date of his return. *"No one knows about that day or hour*, not even the angels in heaven, nor the Son, but only the Father. Be on guard! Be alert! *You do not know when that time will come"* (Mark 13:32-33). When anyone informs the world that he has discovered the time of the Lord's second coming, he immediately reveals himself to be a false prophet.

The "day of the Lord" will come "like a thief in the night" (1 Thess. 5:1). Men will not have predicted that day and have the world waiting in righteous anticipation for it.

Nothing of the kind will happen. Instead, the situation will be similar to the one in Noah's generation when God destroyed the earth with a flood of waters. "For in the days before the flood, people were eating and drinking, marrying and giving in marriage, up to the day Noah entered the ark; and they knew nothing about what would happen until the flood came and took them all away. That is how it will be at the coming of the Son of Man" (Matt. 24:38-39).

Since we cannot determine the day and hour of his coming beforehand, it is our responsibility to be ready always for his return. We must live soberly and righteously. We must watch and pray all the time. We must be busy doing the will of the Lord. Then, whether the Lord returns in the glare of the noonday sun or in the blackness of night, we shall be able to stand before him in confidence and joy.

Events to Accompany His Return

Although we cannot know the exact time of the Lord's return, we can know some of the things which will happen at his second coming. Now we must be careful not to make unwarranted assumptions or to give way to pointless speculation. This has been the downfall of many a Bible student. All we can know with certainty about these events is what is clearly stated in the Word of God. Let us therefore itemize these revealed facts and be content with what God has said.

First, his coming will be spectacular in nature. As the angels said, Christ will come with the clouds. Every eye will see him, and the sound of a great shout and the trump of God will announce the end of time. "For the Lord himself will come down from heaven, with a loud command, with the voice of the archangel and with the trumpet call of God" (1 Thess. 4:16).

Second, the dead will all be raised. "Do not be amazed at this, for a time is coming when all who are in their graves will hear his voice and come out -- those who have done good will rise to live, and those who have done evil will rise to be condemned" (John 5:28-29).

Third, the living will be changed. "Listen, I tell you a mystery: We will not all sleep, but we will all be changed -- in a flash, in the twinkling of an eye, at the last trumpet . . ." (1 Cor. 15:51). Just as the dead will be raised with incorruptible bodies -- since flesh and blood cannot inherit the kingdom of God (1 Cor. 15:50) -- so those who are still alive on the earth at the time of his coming will also have to be changed. Their flesh and blood bodies will have to be miraculously transformed into incorruptible bodies (cf. Phil. 3:21; 1 John 3:2).

At this point it should be pointed out that these first three events -- Christ's spectacular appearance, the raising of the dead, and the changing of the living -- will all occur instantaneously and simultaneously. "In a flash, in the twinkling of an eye, at the last trumpet for (1) the trumpet will sound, and (2) the dead will be raised imperishable, and (3) we will be changed" (1 Cor. 15:52).

Fourth, the Judgment will take place. "When the Son of man comes in his glory, and all the angels with him, he will sit on his throne in heavenly glory. All the nations will be gathered before him . . ." (Matt. 25:31-33). John wrote of the great Judgment Day scene and said: "Then I saw a great white throne and him who was seated on it. Earth and sky fled from his presence, and there was no place for them. And I saw the dead, great and small, standing before the throne, and books were opened. Another book was opened, which is the book of life. The dead were judged according to what they had done as recorded in the books" (Rev. 20:11-12).

It will be Jesus Christ himself who will sit on the great white throne of Judgment (cf. Acts 17:31). Before him will be gathered all men of all generations since the world began. The small and the great, the righteous and the wicked -- all men will be there.

Then, in John's vision of that day, "books were opened." The fact that God is keeping a record of the deeds of men is frequently emphasized in the Scriptures. The record is here represented as being kept in a book (cf. Dan. 7:10). It also seems sure that one of the books to be opened is the Bible, the book which contains the standard by which men's deeds will be judged. Then, according to John, "another book was opened, which is the book of life." The Book of Life is the roll of the names of the righteous (cf. Ex. 32:32; Phil. 4:3). All those whose names are not found in this book will be given over to destruction and torment. (Rev. 13:8).

Finally, says John, "the dead were judged according to what they had done as recorded in the books." Here is a clear statement of what has already been implied, i.e., each man will receive judgment based on "the things done while in the body, whether good or bad" (2 Cor. 5:10).

Fifth, an eternal separation of the righteous from the wicked will be made, and final sentence will be passed on all men. "He will separate the people one from another as a shepherd separates the sheep from the goats. He will put the sheep on his right and but the goats on his left. Then the King will say to those on his right, 'Come, you who are blessed by my Father; take your inheritance, the kingdom prepared for you since the creation of the world. . . .' Then he will say to those on his left, 'Depart from me, you who are cursed, into the eternal fire prepared for the devil and his angels' " (Matt. 25:33-34, 41).

Sixth, the kingdom will be delivered up to the Father. Jesus Christ is now reigning over his kingdom, the church. (Acts 2:34-36). He will continue to reign there until all his enemies are conquered (Acts 2:35). And the last enemy to be conquered is death (1 Cor. 15:24-28). When death is conquered and Christ ceases to reign -- at his second coming -- "then the end will come, when he hands over the kingdom to God the Father" (1 Cor. 15:24). This delivering up of the kingdom is simply the ushering in of the righteous to their eternal reward in the presence of the Father in heaven.

Seventh, the earth will be destroyed. "But the day of the Lord will come like a thief. The heavens will disappear with a roar; the elements will be destroyed by fire, and the earth and everything in it will be laid bare" (2 Pet. 3:10).

Conclusion

Perhaps at no other point does the attitude of modern believers differ more from that of the first-century Christians than with reference to the Lord's second coming. The earliest Christians both desired and expected him to come at any moment. James wrote that "the Lord's coming is near" (James 5:8). The return of Christ was so real, so certain, so sure of fulfillment to these earliest Christians, that they lived with the promise constantly in their minds. How different is this attitude from that of modern-day religious people.

A survey was recently conducted among members of the major denominational bodies in America to determine their position toward certain doctrines of the Christian religion. One of the questions asked was: "Do you believe Jesus will actually return to the earth some day?" Only 44 percent of those persons questioned answered with a definite "Yes."

Men have doubted many of God's promises, but he has never failed to fulfill a single one. And he will not fail to fulfill the sure promise of Christ's second coming. Jesus is coming again. And every generation should be constantly prepared for, believing in, and eagerly awaiting that hour.

What is Christian living all about? It is taking God at his word on all matters and patiently awaiting the fulfillment of his promises at his own appointed times. It is knowing, in particular, that Jesus is coming again to redeem his saints and render vengeance upon his (and their) enemies. It is living each day as if it were our last. It is looking forward to seeing him who died for us.

> When Christ shall come with shout of acclamation
> And take me home, what joy shall fill my heart!
> Then I shall bow with humble adoration
> And there proclaim, My God, how great thou art!

Memorize: 1 Thessalonians 4:16-17

TAKE THOUGHT

1. When James originally wrote this epistle, what circumstances were tempting the Christians to be impatient? What circumstances in our own day subject people to the same temptation?

2. Discuss 2 Peter 3:3-4. Is this prophecy being fulfilled today?

3. What confident assurances of the second coming of Christ do we have? What further assurance could have been given?

4. What series of events will occur at the second coming?

5. How does the attitude of modern Christians toward the return of Christ differ from that of James and his contemporaries?

TAKE ACTION

1. What relationship is there between Christ's resurrection from the dead and his second coming? (cf. 1 Cor. 15:12-19). What evidence do we have to support our faith in his resurrection?

2. Secure a copy of *Who Moved the Stone?* by Frank Morison. With what idea in mind did he begin his research? What change took place as he studied the evidence for Christ's resurrection?

3. Try to get a friend of yours who is not a believer to read *Who Moved the Stone?* and try to use this as a basis for studies with him. Your aim is to lead him to Christ and to prepare him for eternity.

Chapter 12

Some Guidelines for Prayer
James 5:13-18

The great people of God in any generation are those Christians who pray. These people do not necessarily talk most about prayer, advertise their belief in prayer, or try to explain everything about prayer. God's truly great people are those humble and dedicated Christians who actually *take time* and *pray*.

These people have no more time than the rest of us. They just consider prayer more important than the things with which most of us fill our lives. Neither is it that these people are prayerful because they are of a different temperament or personality. They are prayerful because they have disciplined themselves and arranged a workable time, place, and system for prayer. Believing in a God of power who will both hear and answer the petitions of his children, these people have claimed his power through prayer.

Do you pray regularly and fervently each day? Can you truthfully say that communication with God through prayer is a vital part of your life? Not every Christian can preach, lead singing, be a medical missionary, or give great gifts. But there is no Christian who cannot pray. How tragic it is that so many Christians are failing to use this great gift and power.

Since the epistle of James is so practical in its nature, one would naturally expect it to deal with prayer. It does indeed. Some guidelines for prayer are given in James 5:13-18 which need to be studied very carefully.

Some Circumstances Which Call for Prayer

"Is any one of you in trouble? He should pray" (James 5:13a). Whatever one's pain, grief, bereavement, depression, or sorrow, let him pray. When God answers that prayer with needed aid and strength, let that individual not forget to praise God. "Is anyone happy? Let him sing songs of praise" (James 5:13b).

"Is any one of you sick? He should call the elders of the church to pray over him and anoint him with oil in the name of the Lord. And the prayer offered in faith will make the sick person well; the Lord will raise him up" (James 5:14-15a). Turning to what is likely the commonest of troubles, James addresses those who are physically ill. His inspired counsel to such persons is that they call the elders of the church to pray over them and anoint them with oil.

This admonition seems to have been a general one to all Christians concerning all elders, and there is no evidence to support the view that all elders had powers of miraculous healing. Thus the prayer and application of oil must not have been symbolic or sacramental but purely practical. It is always appropriate to have fervent prayers offered for a sick man, for all healing is divine though not necessarily miraculous. Miracles are not possible today, but we are still to pray for the sick and for their healing by the natural agencies (i.e., drugs, treatment, bodily function, etc.) which God is able to employ.

The anointing with oil was simply the practical matter of doing what is within man's power to be an instrument of God in the natural process of healing. It was the equivalent of administering medicine (cf. Luke 10:34). This does not mean, of course, that other medications could never be used.

Is this passage applicable today? Certainly. Elders in the Lord's church are to pray over (i.e., in behalf of) the sick and do what they can in administering to the patient's needs. All this is to be done "in the name of the Lord." The promise is that heaven will respond to such prayers and actions by raising up the sick man.

114

"If he has sinned, he will be forgiven" (James 5:15b). Be careful not to misunderstand this statement. It does not teach that sickness comes to men only as a direct result of their personal sins. It does teach, however, that in times of sickness one may be led to reflect on the fact that he has rejected God in his healthier times and cause him to confess those sins and seek forgiveness.

"Therefore confess your sins to each other and pray for each other so that you may be healed" (James 5:16a). This is the condition of the forgiveness just mentioned. One must be humble enough to confess his sins -- both to God and his brothers -- and pray for pardon. This text does not deal exclusively with "formal confession" made before the entire church, though it certainly includes such. Neither does it prescribe a set manner in which confessions are to be made. They may be made in assembly, to the elders (as this text evidently implies), or by any other convenient means by which the affected parties can be informed of the individual's penitence.

James completes this passage on prayer by citing an example of prayer's power. "The prayer of a righteous man is powerful and effective. Elijah was a man just like us. He prayed earnestly that it would not rain, and it did not rain on the land for three and a half years. Again he prayed, and the heavens gave rain, and the earth produced its crops" (James 5:16b-18). The Old Testament record of these happenings is in 1 Kings 17-18. The point of calling them to mind is to say that Elijah was a mere mortal with the same frailties we have, but God heard him when he prayed. Thus we are assured that God will hear us also if we are righteous and pray in faith.

The Assurances of God Concerning Prayer

Here are only a few passages of Scripture which assure us that God will hear and answer our prayers when we pray according to his will.

"The Lord is near to all who call on him, to all who call on him in truth" (Psa. 145:18).

"The eyes of The Lord are on the righteous and his ears are attentive to their cry. . . . The righteous cry out, and the Lord hears them; he delivers them from all their troubles" (Psa. 34:15,17).

"Ask and it will be given to you; seek and you will find; knock and the door will be opened to you. For everyone who asks receives; he who seeks finds; and to him who knocks, the door will be opened. Which of you, if his son asks for bread, will give him a stone? Or if he asks for a fish will give him a snake? If you, then, though you are evil, know how to give good gifts to your children, how much more will your Father in heaven give good gifts to those that ask him?" (Matt. 7:7-11).

"Again, I tell you, that if two of you on earth agree about anything you ask for, it will be done for you by my Father in heaven. For where two or three come together in my name, there am I with them" (Matt. 18:19-20).

A Christian with a real prayer life is a Christian with God's power in his being. A church filled with devout members who pray in faith will be a great church.

The Need for Prayer

Christians need the help which comes only in answer to prayer. First, prayer will help us to overcome temptation. Satan is real, and he is constantly striving to tempt us into the broad path that leads to destruction. We are constantly warned neither to take his power lightly nor to overestimate our own strength in resisting him (cf. 1 Cor. 10:12). ✓

"But," someone asks, "has not God promised to provide us a way of escape from temptation?" Indeed he has. "No temptation has seized you except what is common to man. And God is faithful; he will not let you be tempted beyond what you can bear. But when you are tempted, he will also provide a way out so that you can stand up under it" (1 Cor. 10:13). This way of escape depends largely on our faithfulness in prayer. Jesus taught us to pray: "And lead us not into temptation, but deliver us from the evil one" (Matt.

6:13). I seriously wonder how many unnecessary temptations we have had to confront and cope with during the past week because we did not pray this petition daily?

Then, in the face of those temptations which we must face, prayer is again the key to escape. Too many of God's people embrace temptation when it comes instead of fleeing to God in prayer. An old and familiar song says:

> Take the name of Jesus ever
> As a shield from every snare;
> If temptations round you gather,
> Breathe that holy name in prayer.

When someone is inviting you into sin or when you are about to lose your temper and sin with your tongue, pray. You need not shout your prayer aloud from the corner of the street -- like the hypocritical Pharisees of Jesus' day. You need not even close your eyes or bow your head or open your mouth. Stare into the eyes of the person provoking you, resolve not to lose your head, and say silently, within your heart, "Oh God, help me. I am so weak but I do not want to sin!" Or, if it is a situation you have no business staying in, turn, and walk away from it -- praying every step of the way for God to keep you from sinning and to help you keep away from such people and situations in the future.

An old adage has it that "Satan trembles when he sees the weakest saint on his knees." Surely it is so. Satan's power to tempt is no match for God's power to strengthen and shield his own. When a saint is praying, he is "plugging in" to divine power which will help give him the victory over temptation.

Second, prayer will help you when you sin. Sometimes you will fail to pray when temptation comes. Sometimes you will not resist Satan as strongly as you should or flee from his enticements to sin. What then? Repent and pray (cf. Acts 8:22). Pray as David did so long ago: "Have mercy on me, O God, according to your unfailing love; according to your great compassion blot out my transgressions. Wash away all my iniquity, and cleanse me from my sin" (Psa. 51:1-2).

Pray that prayer once -- and only once. Keep praying for God to keep you from such sins in the future, but do not keep praying for him to forgive you of a sin in the past. God is anxious to forgive us when we repent and pray and does not have to be begged every day for a week. Pray for him to forgive you and get off your knees in the confidence that he has. Accept forgiveness.

Third, prayer will help a Christian make right decisions and discern God's will for his life. "If any of you lacks wisdom, he should ask God, who gives generously to all without finding fault, and it will be given him" (James 1:5). Knowledge is the possession of facts and information; wisdom is the ability to judge properly with respect to such data. God has given us intelligent minds with which to get facts. We need more than that. If we are Christians, we want and need the ability to weigh those facts in the light of God's will in order to determine the decision or course of action he would have us take. This wisdom comes in answer to prayer. Of the exact manner in which we are given such wisdom, James has no comment. He does affirm, however, that it happens in response to prayer; we accept that truth by faith.

All of us have problems to solve and decisions to make. Young people agonize over the college they should attend or the career they should choose. They select their mates for marriage. They face personal dilemmas at school or with friends and cannot decide what to do. These are things about which young people should pray. Pray for wisdom.

Older people face decisions about changing jobs, moving to a new community, rearing their children, and countless other matters. Use your intellect to get all the information you can about the matter at hand. Then pray for God to give you the wisdom to evaluate it and act so as to do what is pleasing to him. God gives wisdom to those who ask for it.

Think how many foolish mistakes and unwise decisions you have made simply because you did not pray. Learn to take everything to God in prayer and to ask his guidance. Your life will change for the better.

Fourth, prayer will help you render effective service to God. No Christian should ever undertake to render a service in Jesus' name without praying first. A teacher should pray as she begins to prepare her lesson and as she takes her place before the children she instructs. Before going to visit a sick person, a friend who needs to accept Christ, or a Christian who has fallen away, you should pray. A preacher should pray during his week of preparation and before he mounts the pulpit to preach the Word of God.

There is no honorable thing a child of God does in his or her life that is inappropriate as a subject for prayer. Job decisions. Buying a house. Health. Since one's entire life is lived under Christ and to God's glory, everything done in that life should be undergirded by prayer.

Fifth, prayer will help you in times of trouble and sorrow. People who know God through prayer react to trouble and sorrow in a different manner than others. Whereas many people (and even some Christians) cry out in despair when sorrow comes, those who can pray feel and demonstrate a serene strength which comes only from being near to God.

The Word of God assures us of heaven's eagerness to provide mercy and help for Christians in their times of stress and trial. "For we do not have a high priest who is unable to sympathize with our weaknesses, but we have one who has been tempted in every way, just as we are -- yet was without sin. Let us then approach the throne of grace, with confidence, so that we may receive mercy and find grace to help us in time of need" (Heb. 4:15-16).

Conclusion

Until we learn to pray, we will be deprived of so many blessings which otherwise we could have and use to the glory of God and to our own spiritual development. James wrote: "Ye have not, because ye ask not" (James 4:2b).

Henry Ford once bought a million-dollar insurance policy on his life. A good friend of his, who was in the insurance business, asked why he had not bought the policy from him. The answer came back, "You didn't ask!" How many good things of God are we missing simply because we do not pray?

What is Christian living all about? It is learning to live in constant communion with God. It is praying "continually" (1 Thess. 5:17). It is calling upon God in the confidence that one's needs will be generously supplied. It is confessing our weakness and sinfulness, acknowledging our dependence upon God, and submitting to his way.

Memorize: Matthew 6:6

TAKE THOUGHT

1. Who are some of the outstanding Old Testament characters whose lives were marked by prayer? Who are some New Testament characters?

2. How seriously do Christians of your acquaintance take James 5:14-15? Does God work miracles today? Can we pray for miracles? What should we pray for concerning the sick?

3. In what ways can prayer help the Christian?

4. Study the model prayer of Matthew 6:9-13. In what ways is this prayer a model for our own?

5. How much time do you spend in prayer each day?

TAKE ACTION

1. Ask one of the elders of the congregation to come to your class and to lead you in a "prayer meeting." Discuss people (e.g., sick, missionaries, etc.) and situations (e.g., benevolent program, gospel meeting, etc.) which are of concern to you and pray about them.

2. Do some careful study of the Bible on the subject of why some prayers go unanswered. Have a class discussion period on this topic.

Chapter 13

You Are Your Brother's Keeper
James 5:19-20

The theme of the book of James is the day-to-day living of one's religion. This inspired epistle shows, in the most practical terms possible, what Christian living is all about. It instructs Christians in the truth about trials, the use of the tongue, hearing and doing the will of God, loving our neighbors, etc.

Now the epistle closes with another most practical matter: *What if some brother departs from these truths about Christian living?* "My brothers, if one of you should wander from the truth and someone should bring him back, remember this: Whoever turns a sinner from the error of his way will save him from death and cover over a multitude of sins" (James 5:19-20).

The Bible plainly teaches that Christians can backslide (i.e., go backward instead of forward in their spiritual lives). Satan does not give up on a person when he becomes a Christian. If anything, he becomes all the more intent on destroying him. He is the enemy of all God's people and "Prowls around like a roaring lion looking for someone to devour" (1 Pet. 5:8). Therefore Paul warned the Corinthians against falling (1 Cor. 10:12). In the case of some Christians of Galatia, the same apostle said, "You have fallen away from grace" (Gal. 5:4).

A terrible fate awaits the child of God who errs from the truth and does not repent of his sin. "If they have escaped the corruption of the world by knowing our Lord and Savior Jesus Christ and are again entangled in it and overcome, they are worse off at the end than they were in the beginning. It would have been better for them not to have known the way of righteousness, than to have known it and then turn their backs on the sacred commandment that was passed on to them" (2 Pet. 2:20-21).

Yes, an apostate Christian has a more severe fate awaiting him than the man who never obeyed the gospel. There are degrees of punishment to be meted out to the lost (cf. Luke 12:41-48), and those who will receive the greater punishments are people who, having been saved, turn back to the world and its sinful ways.

Not enough attention is being given to this problem in the church. Pulpits should ring with warnings. New converts should be instructed carefully and exhorted in the faith. Fervent prayers should go up for those who are weak, worldly, or wayward. Every effort must be made to reach and restore brothers and sisters who have erred from the truth.

The New Testament makes it clear that Christians are their brothers' keepers. We have a responsibility to lovingly exhort an erring brother back to the Lord. "Brothers, if someone is caught in a sin, you who are spiritual should restore him gently. But watch yourself, or you also may be tempted" (Gal. 6:1).

James was concerned that those who backslide should be restored to faithfulness. Thus he closes his epistle with an appeal to that end.

A Close Look at the Text

"My brothers, if one of you should wander from the truth . . ." Spiritual truth is synonymous with the Scripture, the Word of God (cf. John 17:17). In particular, the New Testament is the Christian's rule of faith and practice. The importance of truth to the child of God is constantly emphasized in the Bible. We must love it (2 Thess. 2:10). We must obey it (Gal. 5:7). We must display its fruits in our daily lives (2 Cor. 4:2).

To "wander from the truth" can involve either or both of the following: (1) accepting a false doctrine instead of holding to the truth or (2) refusing to live by the demands of truth and thus to be guilty of some sinful act of misconduct. In either case, the plight of the individual involved is desperate. Falsehoods and sin lead to death and damnation. Only truth and one's obedience to it can purify and save. He must be turned from his error and brought back to the truth.

"... *And someone bring him back.*" We usually think of conversion as the initial winning of a man to Christ. But the word basically means "turn" and can also be properly applied to the winning back of a Christian who has fallen away. Yes, the erring Christian must be turned around and brought back to the truth. But who will be the one to render this spiritual service to him? Only a Christian who is still loyal to the Savior is in position to reclaim him for Christ.

"*Remember this: Whoever turns a sinner from the error of his way will save him from death...*" An erring child of God who persists in his sin is under sentence of death, for "if we deliberately keep on sinning after we have received the knowledge of the truth, no sacrifice for sins is left, but only a fearful expectation of judgment and of raging fire that will consume the enemies of God" (Heb. 10:26-27). To bring such a person to repentance is to save him from death.

"...*And cover over a multitude of sins.*" Whose sins shall be covered (i.e., put away) by such action? Certainly those of the erring Christian who has repented. And also those sins of neglect which his brother would have incurred if someone had not brought him back (cf. James 4:17).

This is a very important work of the church. If it is the case that our Lord is "not willing that any should perish," how can his people be unconcerned when some brother or sister turns back from Christ and the church? Some of your friends and former classmates in your Bible study group are no longer faithful Christians. How much concern does that fact cause you? What have you done to reach and restore them? What can you do now?

Christian Duty Toward an Erring Brother

Consider what the Bible teaches concerning the duty of a Christian toward his erring brethren.

First, we are obligated by love to *pay attention* to the needs of our brethren. "Each of you should look not only to your own interests, but also to the interests of others" (Phil. 2:4). Out in the world men are selfish and look upon others as enemies or competitors who are to be pushed aside. In the church, the spirit of men must be not to push others down or to delight in their fall but to help others along and to lift them if they should fall.

Now this does not mean that we ought to be nosey or that we have a right to pry into people's lives. But it does mean that when some open and clear signal of weakness is detected in the life of a brother -- and no one becomes a backslider without giving some clear indications of weakness such as absence from services, a critical spirit toward his brothers, or apathy toward the work of the church -- we must not ignore that signal. We must be ready to render immediate aid.

Second, we must *pray* for such persons. We cannot, of course, pray for God to forgive their unfaithfulness until they actually repent. But we can and should pray that God help us bring them to repentance. We can pray that they be spared further temptations which might cause them to become even more deeply involved in sin. If we have the love we should for such people, we cannot refrain from sincere prayer on their behalf.

Third, we must actually *go to the backslider* and appeal for him to come back to the Lord. There is a right way and a wrong way to make that approach. One must never go to such a person with the self-righteous spirit of the ancient Pharisees lest he repulse and drive away the one he intended to reclaim. Instead, he must be humble, sincere, and loving.

He must discuss the person's problems in the strictest confidence. He must do whatever is within his power to advise the backslider from the Word of God and to help him reestablish a right relationship with Christ and the church.

What the Erring One Must Do

After one has done all he can to reclaim a brother, the one who has erred from the truth must himself make the final and decisive move which will restore him to a place of security within the grace of God. What he must do is illustrated in the Parable of the Prodigal Son: "When he came to his senses, he said, 'How many of my father's hired men have food to spare, and here I am starving to death! I will set out and go back to my father and say to him: Father, I have sinned against heaven, and against you. I am no longer worthy to be called your son; make me like one of your hired men.' So he got up and went to his father" (Luke 15:17-20a).

First, the erring Christian must *"come to his senses."* He must admit his lost and unhappy plight. He must yearn for home and his heavenly Father. He must repent of having sinned against the Father and against the rest of his Father's family.

Second, he must *resolve to go back* to the Father and his brethren. No more "Well, I know what I should do but . . ." type of hesitation and holding back. There must be a firm decision. Like the prodigal son, he must say, "I will get up and go to my father."

Third, he must *carry out his resolve* immediately. No amount of resolutions or good intentions can replace the actual return home. He must go back to the place he left, the place where his Father is, the church. He cannot stay away from the church and be saved. He cannot be out of fellowship with the church and in fellowship with the Father, for the church is the family of God (1 Tim. 3:15).

125

Fourth, he must *confess his sins* and ask forgiveness. No excuses, rationalizations, or attempts to justify what has happened. No saying, "If I have sinned, I ask to be forgiven." The prodigal son said, "Father, I have sinned against heaven, and against you. I am no longer worthy to be called your son" (Luke 15:21). This is the only appropriate sentiment for one who has run away from home and is coming back in penitence.

The Church's Duty Toward the Impenitent

A final consideration with regard to reclaiming the erring involves the church's duty toward those brethren who refuse to repent of their errors in doctrine or life.

The Lord wants his church to be "a radiant church, without stain or wrinkle or any blemish, but holy and blameless" (Eph. 5:27). Therefore the church cannot tolerate deliberate sin among its membership. If a congregation chooses to permit impure and impenitent persons to remain undisciplined within its fellowship, it thereby becomes a partaker of their wickedness (cf. Rev. 2:20).

Sometimes this thought is expressed when elders urge members of a congregation to speak to and exhort certain backsliding brethren: "But since we all sin and are far from being perfect, how can we 'throw stones' at others?" There is an obvious world of difference between Christians who sin through weakness and those who sin deliberately. Those who recognize their own imperfection and confess their sins daily are commanded to take action toward those who sin and show no sign of repentance. Even a weak and carnal church like the one at Corinth was told to do something about its unruly members who would not repent (cf. 1 Cor. 15).

When there is a brother in the church who is in sin and impenitent over his condition, the elders have a duty to lead the church in attempting to bring him to repentance. If he will not repent, they must take the lead in disfellowshipping him. The whole congregation must participate in the process and support the action or it will not have the desired effect.

The purpose of the action is not to hurt the person in question but to save his soul by impressing him with the seriousness of his condition and his urgent need of remorse and reconciliation. Paul commanded the Corinthians to "hand this man over to Satan [i.e., refuse him fellowship and privilege within the church] so that the sinful nature may be destroyed [i.e., so that he will be caused to repent of whatever works of the flesh are in his life], and his spirit saved on the day of the Lord Jesus" (1 Cor. 5:5).

The Lord has even told us the exact procedure to follow in such cases: (1) go to the erring brother and plead for his repentance, (2) if he refuses take two or three witnesses and approach him again, (3) if he still will not repent present his case before the entire assembly, and (4) if that fails exclude him from the fellowship of the church (Matt. 18:15-17).

The discipline of the disorderly is not pleasant, but it is commanded of the saints (2 Thess. 3:6) and is necessary for the purity of the church (cf. Heb. 3:12-13).

Conclusion

Let every child of God resolve in his heart not to be among that number who err from the truth. Let us resolve to live a godly and faithful Christian life. Let us live so as to be able to say: "But we are not of those who shrink back and are destroyed, but of those who believe and are saved" (Heb. 10:39).

Beyond this, let every child of God resolve to love his brothers and sisters in the Lord to the degree that he will attempt to encourage those who are following Christ faithfully in their daily lives and to reclaim those brethren who have erred from the truth so as to save their souls from death.

What is Christian living all about? It is taking heed first to one's own heart and life to guard his own commitment to Jesus as Lord. It is looking then to the spiritual needs of others who are children of God but who are struggling under a heavy load of difficulties and discouragements. It is loving these people enough to stand with them and bear some of their burdens. It is lifting those who have already fallen beneath the weight and walking with them until they have recovered their spiritual strength in the Lord. It is by this means that the world will know that we truly are Christ's disciples and will desire to follow One who can produce such a spirit among his followers (cf. John 13:34-35).

Memorize: Galatians 6:1-2

TAKE THOUGHT

1. Can a Christian fall away from Christ and the church? Will he be lost?

2. What are some common factors involved when people do fall away from the faith? What can we do in the local church to strengthen new converts and weak Christians?

3. What is our obligation to an erring brother? What attitude must underlie our efforts? (cf. Gal. 6:1).

4. What is the obligation of the erring Christian himself?

5. What must the church's action be when an erring Christian remains impenitent? How generally practiced is this commandment?

TAKE ACTION

1. Who are some of your friends who are no longer faithful to Christ? What can you do to help them?

2. Study Hebrews 10:24 and suggest some specific things you can do to accomplish its requirement.

CPSIA information can be obtained
at www.ICGtesting.com
Printed in the USA
BVHW061717170419
545808BV00013B/262/P

785 409 3652